CATHERINE & IGOR STRAVINSKY

Boosey & Hawkes London 1973

Library of Congress Catalogue Card No. 72-95737

ISBN: 0-85162-008-6

Colour Photographs © Copyright 1973 by Theodore Stravinsky
Photographic prints by François Martin, Geneva
Designed by Derek Birdsall
Printed in England by Westerham Press

CATHERINE & IGOR STRAVINSKY

a family album by Theodore Stravinsky

7/50   Th. Stravinsky

To the memory of my father

Author's Note

Without being too arbitrary the life of my father Igor Stravinsky
can, I think, be divided into three distinct parts.

The first lasts until 1920 and forms the subject of this album. It
could be entitled 'from Russia to the West'.

The second would correspond to the life of the composer and his
family in France, from 1920–1939.

The third, from 1939 to his death in 1971, would cover the years
that my father spent in the United States.

It is exclusively the first part of this long life that these short notes
seek to evoke rather than to narrate. Gravitating round a group of
childhood memories – things that I saw or experienced and have
remained in my memory, confirmed by what I heard directly from
my parents about my family – they accompany a selection of
family photographs, mostly unpublished and coming to me from
my mother. Text and photographs together form a kind of series of
flashbacks illustrating my father's family life up to 1920 and thus
covering the period of my own childhood. And so it is not to be
wondered at if music occupies only a marginal place in these pages.
My father's works will only be quoted in them as forming
chronological landmarks.

Finally five photographs, taken by my wife at Evian towards the end
of August 1970, only a few months before my father's death, make
a heartrending epilogue to this 'Family Album'.

Igor and Catherine Stravinsky, my parents, at the heart of my childhood memories

At the end of the last century Feodor Ignatievich and Anna Kyrillovna, the parents of Igor Stravinsky, played an integral part in the musical circles of St. Petersburg, which was then capital of Russia.

Feodor Ignatievich (Theodore son of Ignatius), born in 1843, came from an old Polish family and made a career as basso cantante at the Maryinsky Theatre, the imperial opera house. A voice of very large range and warm, attractive quality coupled with exceptional dramatic gifts very soon won him a great reputation. A man without preconceptions, he set himself to rid the venerable St. Petersburg stage of the dust accumulated by archaic routine, and his introduction of a lively, realistic style of acting made him a real innovator. Theodore Stravinsky, my grandfather, was to make a strong personal mark on the Russian operatic stage of his day. As a litterateur of taste, he also made an important collection of books.

His wife, Anna Kyrillovna (Anne, daughter of Cyril), born Kholodovsky, possessed a pretty mezzo-soprano voice but did not use her voice professionally, contenting herself with singing for her own pleasure. She was a good musician, of whom her son Igor was later to say: 'It was from her that I inherited the valuable ability to read orchestral scores at sight'.

It was an exemplary marriage, but as parents Theodore and Anna Stravinsky were perhaps too demanding; and they encountered quite a number of difficulties in the education of their four hot-headed sons: Roman, Youri, Igor and Gouri. Warm family ties bound these boys to their numerous Yellachich and just as numerous Nossenko cousins, and every summer brought high-spirited family gatherings at the country estate of one family or the other.

It was in St. Petersburg, the Tsar's handsome capital with its Palladian architecture, that Igor and his brothers spent their childhood and youth. Igor was to make his law studies there – in obedience to his parents' reasonable wishes – and his musical studies in answer to the overriding demands of his own sole inclination. It was in St. Petersburg too, that Igor Feodorovich Stravinsky and Ekaterina Gavrilovna Nossenko (Catherine, daughter of Gabriel), his cousin, united their destinies on 24 January 1906; there that they spent the first three years of their married life and that their two first children – Theodore and Ludmila – were born, 1907–1908.

1910. A winter's day and a young man of 27, bending over the pale little boy of not quite three as I was then, laughing and singing in strict time '*Down it goes, down it goes, the glass of beer*' to make him swallow the brimming spoonful of bull's blood prescribed by the doctor. Every meal the game was repeated and the revolting event turned to a musical occasion. A devoted father already, Igor was touchingly attentive to his firstborn. That is the first memory that, more than sixty years later, I have of my father, Igor Stravinsky.

No earlier memory, but a droll little story that my father himself told me. When I was born, my mother was unable to feed me and a wet nurse had to be found without delay. In answer to an advertisement my father went to an employment agency and there was presented with several young women, drawn up in a row with their breasts bared. One after the other each of these squirted a few drops of her precious liquid into a little glass, which was handed to the young father for his appreciation. I do not know what his method of judging was, but the successful candidate seems to have given complete satisfaction.

The rigours of winter in that great northern city often seem interminable, while summer with its melting 'white nights' passes like a dream. This was not the climate to suit my mother's delicate health and very soon my father was forced to take this into consideration. The apartment on the Anglissky Prospekt was not to remain the young couple's home for long, and in 1910 it was decided to leave the banks of the Neva. After that date my father was only to return there by himself and only to stay for short periods in connection with his work. The family was to go on growing – there were already nannies, governesses, uncles, aunts and grandmothers – and was to lead until 1914 a constantly shifting, nomad existence. Igor and Catherine had just built a summer country-house at Ustilug in Volhynia in the extreme southwest of Russia on land belonging to my mother and her sister Ludmila. Every summer until 1913 this was to be our family home until the autumn came and the weather broke, when the whole household would move to a warmer climate in the West – Switzerland or the French Riviera. And so it was that my very early years were a perpetual coming and going between St. Petersburg and Ustilug, Ustilug and La Baule, Clarens, Beaulieu, Ustilug, Clarens . . . I should like to halt a moment at Ustilug, which was the scene of the most exquisite of my earliest memories. Things and events now begin to stand out more clearly in my memory.

Summers at Ustilug were my delight and in retrospect they cast a happy light over my whole childhood.

The newly planted trees made a cool, light shade round the house itself. Only a wooden fence separated us from our cousins Ira and Gania, son and daughter of my mother's sister Ludmila who had married a naval officer, Gregory Belyankin. The close bond of affection uniting my mother and her sister formed the vital link between the two families. The two households had built houses next door to each other. Ours was sober, but the Belyankin's flanked by a square tower and a semi-circular gallery or verandah (never in fact finished), seemed to me the height of magnificence – moreover behind this mysterious place there was a fenced enclosure inside which four enormous St. Bernard dogs seemed to be always on the watch for something. And then there was my uncle's fascinating Dedion-Bouton, with its spluttering engine and enormous brass headlamps. I always felt a sense of humiliation that my parents did not possess one. With what rapture I used to manipulate the enormous rubber bulb of the horn, deafening the grown-ups' sensitive ears! Hoisted up on a moleskin seat by the side of my uncle, I was in ecstasy as we made our way in the teeth of the wind around the lawn at a speed that seemed to me breakneck. In front of our own house, on the other hand, and beneath my father's windows, the rule was silence. I used to love to slip into his study, a big square room whose smallest details are still clear in my mind. The picture-covered walls, the tall desk, the Empire writing-table with the big drawers, pens and pencils, rulers and India rubbers, different coloured inks in their small glass bottles, erasers of all shapes and sizes, Japanese paper-weights . . . The attraction exercised by all these things was all the greater because one was strictly forbidden to touch them! It was in this sanctum of my father's, where everything filled me with wonder and through the agency of a print, that I one day made my first acquaintance with Alexander Pushkin. Standing in front of the poet's portrait, my father explained to me who this gentleman was, what being a writer meant. 'Pushkin' means, in Russian, 'of or belonging to a cannon'; and it was that which impressed me most. On the grand piano, at which my father had lately composed *Fireworks* for the marriage of Rimsky-Korsakov's daughter, there was always the score at which he was working. Had not his old master one day answered his young pupil's question whether he was right to compose at the piano by saying: 'Some

compose at the piano, others away from it. Well, you'll be one who composes at the piano'. Prompted by an overriding need to feel himself in direct contact with sound itself Stravinsky, as is well known, was to compose at the piano all his life.

At Ustilug, far removed from any intellectual centre, the family (large enough now, in all conscience) was inevitably thrown back on to its own resources. I only remember one new face there – that of Stepan Mitusov, a great friend of my father's who had collaborated with him in the libretto for *The Nightingale*. At Ustilug Stravinsky was to finish the score of *Fire Bird* in spring 1910. In fact the composer himself said that Ustilug was for him the ideal place to compose.

In the neighbourhood, which was entirely rural, there were a great many Jews, all of whom lived in very modest conditions. At harvest time they could be seen camping in the surrounding orchards in big tents. One day a pretty, smiling girl called Raissa rang the bell. I can still see mother opening the door to her, whereupon I found myself, to my amazement, face to face with the open beaks of two wild-eyed chickens, bound together by the legs; for Raissa had come to sell her poultry. My surprise was even greater when I raised my eyes and saw the girl's strange head-dress – a sort of cap painted with red hair. I could not wait to have this explained to me . . . and my father eventually told me that in this part of the country Jewish girls shaved their heads for their wedding-day, and that those who could not afford a real wig made do with a linen cap on which they carefully painted a head of hair with a middle parting.

Every year, as the summer came to an end, the preparations for departure caused a general fever of activity in the family. Parents, grandmothers, nannies and governesses spent their days doing up suitcases, shutting trunks, strapping up Japanese hampers, not forgetting those marvellous hatboxes – unknown to children nowadays – which the fashions of *la belle époque* had swollen to enormous dimensions. Then Igor would gather the whole family, and there was a silence. An ancient Russian custom demands that, when a whole family leaves a place to which they wish to return, they must all sit together for a moment in which to recollect oneself for a few seconds – *prisyest* as it is called in Russian – and sign themselves with the cross as they rise. This was a universal custom in Russia in those days and my parents followed it gladly. Despite our excitement we children felt these few moments to be very solemn . . . but very long!

Now trunks and suitcases are already piled on the steps outside. We take our seats in the various carriages. The horses whinny and paw the ground. A crack of the whip gives the signal for departure . . . and good-bye Ustilug until next year! After several hours jolting we were at Vladimir-Volhynsk, then in the evening Kovel. It was quiet at night, under the starry sky, and the echo of our footsteps on the wooden pavements of the little town made me rather frightened, until I was reassured by the grip of my father's hand on mine. At the hotel my mother was careful to sprinkle the sheets with some yellow powder 'to get rid of the fleas'; it was all part of the fun of travelling. Next morning the little station, cool with an early autumn tang in the air, and then the wheezing train to Warsaw. Waiting there for the express to Berlin, we were given tea at the station buffet, where I could not take my eyes off the enormous chromium-plated samovar, shaped like a railway engine and emitting clouds of steam. On the platform mother and father checked and re-checked the luggage, while the rest of us found our places in the well-upholstered carriages of the international express, with its gold-braided staff.

Twenty-four hours in Berlin, a day always made memorable by a visit to the Tiergarten and another, hardly less exciting, to the toy department of a big store. It was there that, after much preliminary trying on, I was bought my first sailor-suit, much to my satisfaction. My father, defying all the rules of hygiene, tried a whole series of whistles – much to my mother's embarrassment and to my delight, although the stares of the shopgirls made me uncomfortable – until he found the shrillest of them all, which he pinned on to my new sailor-suit, like a decoration. On that occasion there was suddenly a great stir in the shop. From the street outside could be heard the sound of an unusual car-horn, and everyone rushed to the doors and the windows. My father hoisted me on his shoulders, so that I too could see the big white open car as it passed and the serious-looking gentleman waving his greetings to the crowd. It was the Kaiser.

My father's growing reputation, young though he still was, brought the whole staff of the Edition Russe de Musique which had its headquarters in Berlin, to see him off at the station, and this meant a grand distribution of Berlin sweets among us children.

Next stage Paris, and a night at the Hotel d'Egypte in the Rue des Pyramides. High on the chimney-piece the solemn black marble clock, its gilded face flanked by two brass sphinxes, had a loud tick which at last overcame my youthful traveller's excitement and I was eventually allowed the great treat of sleeping in my parents' bed.

The train once more . . . and at last La Baule! After the interminable journey we had hardly reached our destination when my father allowed himself the delight of introducing his son at once to the vast ocean and giving him his first taste of sea-water. Neither of my cousins nor my small sister were given the privilege of this initiation. They had stayed with the grown-ups doing the unpacking. I can still hear the cry of the waffle-seller on the beach – '*Arrivez papas, arrivez mamans, faites plaisir à vos enfants*' The dwelling we had taken for the last weeks of the summer was a chocolate-coloured chalet standing in a pinewood. There my father was to compose his *Deux Poèmes de Verlaine*, for baritone and piano, dedicated to his brother Gouri, who was a singer like their father. This uncle was at La Baule with us. After a few weeks we all went to Switzerland, and on 23 September 1910 my mother gave birth to her third child, my brother Sviatoslav-Soulima, at Lausanne.

The winter was spent at Beaulieu-sur-Mer. An apartment on the first floor and immediately beneath – what luck! – a confectioner's where we ate sugared violets and sugared mimosa-blossoms. My father was working at *Petrushka*, and while he was composing scenes of popular rejoicing in the setting of a dark, wintry St. Petersburg, under his windows the Beaulieu carnival masks passed backwards and forwards in the bright Mediterranean sunshine. In the evening my father took my mother and my aunts to see the procession, and next morning my sister and I and our two cousins spent our time on all fours picking up the myriad-coloured confetti from the floor of our apartment.

Still at Beaulieu I can see two enormous and glittering golden vestments, clouds of incense filling the dining-room and a great copper basin full of water, hear the chanting and feel in my hands the big lighted candle! Everything seemed so beautiful to me! It is our small brother's christening. Both Mother and Father always had a deep respect for holy things and for the ceremonies and traditions of the Orthodox Church. With the years their faith grew deeper and deeper and even my father, whom circumstances later hindered from religious practice, preserved deep in his heart an unaltered faith.

A little later, at the end of spring, my father spent a short time in Rome, where he finished *Petrushka*, returned to his family and we all set out again for Ustilug and the beautiful Ukraine summer, with its juicy fruit and the white strawberries smelling of pineapple. One more child . . . one more nanny!

It was at this time that Stravinsky sketched a cantata for male voice choir and orchestra *Le Roi des Etoiles*, dedicated to Claude Debussy, and composed a diptych for voice – *Deux Poèmes de Balmont*, *Forget-me-not* and *The Dove* dedicated respectively to his mother and his sister-in-law, Ludmila Belyankin. But before all else he was working again on an idea that had been haunting him since long before *Petrushka* – *The Rite of Spring*.

Once again the first autumn frosts dispersed our whole little world and this time it was to the shores of the Lake of Geneva: Clarens and the Pension les Tilleuls.

Every time that we moved house for a few weeks my father always managed to give an air of permanence to what was in fact very temporary, and to make sure of the isolation that he found indispensable to his work. All his life, wherever he might be, he always surrounded himself with his own atmosphere. The most anonymous hotel room would be given a personal touch, as it were a sign-manual of his personality. His passion of the moment would be displayed on the walls, whether it was a magnificent antique or an *image d'Epinal*. During the years I am speaking of the place of honour was reserved for Japanese prints, something that European connoisseurs were discovering, or rediscovering, with delight; and Stravinsky was to compose his *Trois Poésies de la lyrique japonaise* for high voice and piano; *Akahito*, dedicated to Maurice Delage, *Mazatsumi* to Florent Schmitt and *Tsaraiuki* to Maurice Ravel.

I can still see leaning by my father's side on the wrought-iron balcony outside our windows at the Hôtel du Châtelard a little man, perfectly turned out, with glowing eyes, tufted eyebrows and a fine head of slightly silvering hair. I can still hear them whistling a short phrase five, ten, fifteen times to the blackbirds in the garden who, to my childish delight, ended by whistling the same phrase back to them. The little man was none other than Maurice Ravel.

A common taste for Japanese art and the similarity of their researches into aesthetics at that time formed the substance of the friendship between Ravel and Stravinsky. In the spring of 1913 they were for a time neighbours and saw each other every day. Only the railway track separated the Hôtel des Crêtes, where the French composer was staying from the Hôtel du Châtelard (since demolished)

where the Russian composer was living with his family. He had come to Clarens in search of a climate that suited his young wife's health, and Ravel, who had his mother with him, was simply returning to his father's native country. Perhaps there is some destiny connecting this part of the world with musicians. Mendelssohn spent a long time here, Tchaikovsky wrote his *Maid of Orleans* here and in our own time Paul Hindemith was to spend his last years in the neighbourhood. It was here, at the Hôtel du Châtelard, that Stravinsky completed *The Rite of Spring*.

And here let us stop a moment and consider. Is not the astounding creative vitality of this young thirty-year-old musician a matter for wonder? In three years (1910–1913) he has written the three masterpieces that are to place him at the peak of his reputation – *Firebird*, *Petrushka* and *The Rite of Spring* – and at the same time, as we have seen, like any patriarch, he has made ample provision for the upkeep of a family living in a perpetual state of nomadism. He has even found time for a multiplicity of additional personal journeys to meet Diaghilev and his company in Paris, in Rome or in Bayreuth. The stormy first night of the *Rite* was, as is well known, on 29 May 1913, at the Théâtre des Champs-Elysées in Paris and a few days later an attack of typhoid contracted and nursed in the French capital, seemed at one moment to be about to take a dramatic turn, deeply alarming to the composer's friends and relations.

The summer was spent by the whole family again at Ustilug, as always. To amuse himself during his convalescence the composer wrote *Souvenirs de mon enfance*, three small pieces for voice and piano dedicated to his three children, Theodore, Ludmila and Sviatoslav-Soulima. Twenty years later he was to transcribe them for a small instrumental ensemble.

Back to Clarens in the autumn. But who could have imagined that we were leaving Russia for ever and that we should never see Ustilug again? On 15 January 1914 my sister Milena, my parents' fourth and last child, was born at Lausanne. My mother who was suffering from exhaustion after the birth of her child, was ordered to spend some time in the mountains, at Leysin. My father accompanied her, showing the care and solicitude characteristic of him whenever there was any question of his family's health. It was at Leysin that the real friendship between my parents and Jean Cocteau began – I say real because, in spite of many rough patches, irritations and even occasional eclipses this friendship never failed and was one day to lead, in the most natural way in the world, to a close collaboration in a great stage work – *Oedipus Rex* (1926).

In 1914 my parents decided not to return for the summer to Ustilug as usual, but to remain in the Swiss mountains; but they had no inkling that this decision, taken purely on temporary grounds of health, was to have consequences that were to determine the whole future course of their lives. It was after they had left Leysin and transported the whole family to the little summer resort of Salvan en Valais (Pension Bel-Air) that the First World War broke out. As he was not subject to mobilisation my father was not obliged to return to Russia; and so it happened that he was not to see his native country again until 48 years later, after his eightieth birthday.

On 26 May *The Nightingale* had at last had its first performance, in Paris, after remaining unfinished for a long period after it was begun in St. Petersburg during 1908. My father's workroom at Salvan was decorated at this time with the maquettes for this opera, presented by their designer Alexandre Benois to his friend Igor Stravinsky. At Salvan, too, he was to compose *Pribautki* with his brother Gouri's voice in mind; and the *Three Pieces for String Quartet*. One day at Salvan my parents' gloomy and worried look made me realise that something very serious was happening. My grandmother was with us at the time and it was plain that she was very upset as she explained to me: 'They say that it means war!' A few days later even neutral Switzerland declared a general mobilisation, and every day there was shooting practice in the field opposite our pension. My small friends and I had soon invented a game with the empty cartridge-cases that we proudly picked up. At mealtimes in the pension my father was forced to invent every kind of subterfuge in order to avoid the all-enveloping theories of a formidable and celebrated theosophical lady . . . and we were strictly forbidden to accept her continual offers of delicious gingerbread spread with jam!

When autumn came, we went back to Clarens, not to the hotel this time but to a villa rented from Ernest Ansermet. Close ties were formed at this time between my father and him, and Ansermet was of course to play an important part in making Stravinsky's early works known all over the world. It was in this commonplace little villa of La Pervenche that my father began work on one of his most important scores – *Les Noces* (*The Wedding*). This work was often interrupted and taken up again, while the composer completed

a number of other pieces: *Renard, L'Histoire du Soldat, Ragtime, Pulcinella, Concertino, Symphonies for wind instruments, Mavra,* and several lesser things. The final instrumentation of *Les Noces* was only to be determined nine years later.

And so we come to the autumn of 1914, at Clarens, and the sad parting from my grandmother, who had made up her mind to go back to wartime Russia. She had been widowed more than ten years earlier, and since then had divided her time between her apartment in St. Petersburg, which she shared with her youngest son, Gouri, and visits of weeks or months to us at Ustilug, in Switzerland or in France . . . Dashing Uncle Gouri had just volunteered for service on the Balkan front and my grandmother wished to be near him. She had already lost her eldest son, Roman, and both Youri and Igor were married with families of their own, so that all her maternal affection was concentrated on her youngest, Gouri. It was a brave thing to undertake, alone and in wartime, this long, dangerous journey from Switzerland to Russia, which meant travelling through the dangerous area of the Dardanelles. When she reached St. Petersburg – now Leningrad – she was to live through the whole of the revolution and the hard years that followed. The devoted friends of her sons' invented an ingenious ruse by which she could remain unmolested in her apartment, by contriving to have her made the caretaker of her own husband's library, which the new government had declared state property.

After our grandmother's departure our family spent two winter months at Château d'Oex in the Vaudois Alps, staying in the Hotel Victoria. It was nothing less than a miracle that, in the middle of such a restless existence, my parents had been able to create and to preserve a genuine and peaceful family atmosphere for their children. Igor, the solicitous father, although easily exasperated by trifling matters, at one moment so close to us with his warm and reassuring humanity and a moment later beyond our reach in the secret world of his artistic creation . . . By his side Catherine, wife and mother, an exceptionally big-souled woman, gentle and devoted, always there . . .

But the nomadic life that my family had led during my first seven years was soon to come to an end. As the war took on global dimensions, my parents were obliged to think of settling permanently in Switzerland. They were further prompted to such a decision by the problem of their children's education. A number of warm friendships already linked my father to the French-speaking part of

Switzerland, which was to be his base of operations until 1920. In spring 1915 Igor and Catherine in fact rented the Villa Rogivue in the Avenue des Pâquis at Morges, a delightful little town near Lausanne, on the banks of the Lake of Geneva.

They were no sooner settled than the whole house, and not only my father's workroom, began to fill with the trinkets and pieces of furniture collected in the course of visits to the antique-shops of the neighbourhood – happy days when one could still make such amazing finds! Many things which later followed the family in its successive moves were to become for us childhood memories, trinkets and pieces of furniture some of which, to my great delight, are still in my possession after more than 30 years. The eighteenth century Swiss table, for instance, on whose heavy polished pearwood top so many scores were written – from *The Rite of Spring* to the *Dumbarton Oaks Concerto* – was bought at Clarens . . . then the big cupboard covered with primitive polychrome designs and used to hold my father's manuscripts . . . the gouaches of Naples that he brought back from Italy on one occasion . . .

There were no Japanese prints on the walls of the Villa Rogivue at Morges. Their place had been taken by Larionov's vigorous maquettes for *Renard* and by the charming brightly coloured water-colours that my mother was painting at that time to illustrate *Les Noces*. She had a great talent for drawing and had spent several months as a girl with her cousins at the Académie Colarossi in Paris.

Now, too, the figures who had hitherto been to us children nothing but more or less mysterious names pronounced by the grown-ups, or at most shadowy figures glimpsed in hotel corridors, began to become real people. As with all children, our preferences were quickly established. Diaghilev, for instance, with his re-assuringly fat cheeks, soon became 'Uncle Serge'. We used to run to meet him and climb on his lap, knowing that his pockets were always full of sweets for us. Much later my father told me that there was one secret pocket in which this most superstitious of men kept the amulets from which he would never be parted! Nijinsky, with his fragile body and lost look, did not appeal to us, even though mama explained that this gentleman was the greatest dancer in the world and that when he jumped you would think he was flying . . . Father would be closeted for long hours with these two, and through the door we used to hear thunderous chords interrupted by shouts which were some-times so loud that they frightened us. 'They can't be scolding papa,

are they?' said my sister Mika (Ludmila) anxiously. And great was our astonishment and relief when the three grown-ups reappeared smiling.

Diaghilev, Nijinsky, Massine, Larionov, Gontcharova, Prokofiev with a few other friends constituted the world of the Ballets Russes. They had become friends in Russia, and now all of them were forced, like my parents, to suffer the common lot of émigrés. Included in this group of friends was Basil Kibalchich, chorus master. At Morges new friendships were to be formed which would play an equally important part in my father's life. Ernest Ansermet, the writer C. F. Ramuz, the painter René Auberjonois, Henri Bischoff another painter, Jean Morax who was also a painter and his brother the dramaturge René Morax, Alexandre Cingria yet another painter, and Charles-Albert Cingria, this great but little known poet . . . These were the centre of a circle of friends whom my parents were always delighted to welcome to their house and table. Although day-to-day worries were always present, the warm Russian hospitality never flagged, and it would be hard to count the number of friends whom the Stravinskys entertained at Morges.

Although I cannot distinguish them in my mind, I remember with a kind of tender joy our glittering Christmasses and our Russian-style Easters, not to speak of the New Year's Day, when mother and father dressed up to amuse us. The head of the family appeared as a seedy painter, with a Rembrandt cap, Lavallière tie, an easel on his shoulder, and holding brushes and palette.

For us children life was composed of the rhythmic alternation of school-terms and holidays. In the mornings at home everyone went about on tiptoe . . . Stravinsky was composing. But then suddenly the maid would forget the rules and start singing, if it wasn't the cook whistling! No more was needed to unleash the composer's thunder-bolts, and my mother was obliged to use all her tact in order to pacify her husband, . . . and keep her servants! In the afternoons, on the other hand, the atmosphere was more relaxed. My father would generally be orchestrating and my mother spent peaceful hours by his side copying scores or piano arrangements until we got back from school. Then it was time for the Russian lesson. While she was dictating to me or I was reading some passage aloud to her, she would be deftly rolling (I can still see the little instrument she used) my father's favourite cigarettes, made of a tobacco that scented the whole house. He used to smoke them in a long holder made of the beak of an albatross and (as we were told) 'very, very valuable'. We children always spoke Russian with our parents, French at school and among ourselves, and German with the governesses.

Although our family life had now become settled, Stravinsky himself was always travelling. There was no dearth of occasions, all connected with the activities of the Ballets Russes, but the geographical extension of these journeys was severely limited by the war. A real friendship and mutual admiration existed between him and Diaghilev. Father, however, was under no illusions about the temptations in which the world of the Ballets Russes involved him. In a letter written from Ustilug and dated 14.x.1912 he made this astounding confession to his friend Maurice Delage '. . . fame and money are the temptations which gnaw my vitals without my being wholly aware of it . . .' One can also see from this letter that he was under no illusions about the atmosphere of unsavoury intrigue behind the scenes of the illustrious company or of the snobbery to which it owed much of its support. But life is life, his profound nature and his art had from the very beginning of his career made twofold and contradictory claims on Stravinsky. This extraordinarily vital, extroverted man, who really needed direct contact with the musical public, not simply in order to make his music better known, also found in family life the ideal climate for composition. This double psychological need found expression in the constant alternation between a genuine and intimate family life and journeys away from home, first of all for meetings with Diaghilev and his company wherever they might be, and later for concert tours of his own. This 'double life' was to continue until the winter of 1938–9, when he lost first his daughter Ludmila, then his wife and finally his mother, all within six tragic months. With the breaking-up of the home, family ties were to become less close, each of us were to make our own lives and Father, too, when in 1940 he married Vera Sudeikin née de Bosset in the United States.

But we must return to the years 1915–6 at Morges. My father's return home, whether it was from Rome, Madrid or Paris, was always awaited with the greatest eagerness by my mother and us children. On these occasions he never failed to bring back a surprise – like the recording of a bull-fight, with fanfares, olés from the crowd and above all the roaring of the bull which made us hold our breaths, while Father – who for all his slender build was a very muscular man – imitated the movements and gestures of the torero, with a red rug thrown over a stool. It was to commemorate his first visit to Spain that Stravinsky was to write his pianola piece called *Madrid*, which he later orchestrated and included in the *Four Pieces for Orchestra*. Later still his own son Soulima, who had become an excellent pianist, made a two-piano transcription of this *Madrid* of our childhood.

And then there is the 'Espanola' of the *Five Easy Pieces* which evokes irresistibly for me (just as the *Three Easy Pieces*) our first contact with the piano, the first steps, I would say, of our childish fingers on the key-board, the first reading of the notes on the stave. And also the beautiful blue of the walls in my father's study where each of us, in turn, came to sit for twenty minutes at the upright piano on the piano stool, which was always adjusted high enough to prevent us from reaching the pedals, cruel temptation! Our teacher? Father himself, Igor Stravinsky, who showed then with his little pupils an outstanding patience, or better, I think – and I am even certain – mastered a natural impatience. But shall we not find this self-control again in this man who was so impatient in his dealings with the musicians in the orchestra?

One day Father returned from Geneva highly delighted at having unearthed a Hungarian cimbalom, an unusual instrument for which he had been longing to get, as he wanted to use it in the score of *Renard*, on which he was working. He always felt this need of being in direct contact, with the actual material of sound. I can still see the arrival of this unfamiliar object. It was hardly unpacked in the courtyard, where Father showed it to us, before we were quite enchanted by what was not, of course, a child's instrument; and each of us was allowed in turn to christen it. As soon as it had been given its place in my father's workroom, though, no one was allowed to touch it. When he was working on *The Soldier's Tale* he got hold of a whole battery of percussion instruments, among which was a bass drum covered with white and green triangles and almost certainly originating in some local village band in the Canton of Vaud.

On 20 December 1915 Diaghilev organised a gala performance in aid of the International Red Cross in Geneva, the institution's original home. It was a memorable occasion for Stravinsky, who was to conduct for the first time in public. In the programme were an orchestral suite of fragments from *Firebird*, for which he was responsible, while the ballet-music of *Carnaval* (Schumann) and Rimsky-Korsakov's *Midnight Sun* were conducted by Ernest

Ansermet. How surprised, overjoyed and bursting with pride I felt when my parents told me that they would take me with them! I arrived at the theatre in my Sunday suit and patent-leather shoes and at once began to take in every detail with wide open eyes. I was an imaginative little boy, with a strong visual sense, and I saw it all – the curtain, the stage, the hall itself, the big central chandelier, the scarlet plush and the gilt. When the hall was dark and the stage lit by the foot-lights, I saw my mother sitting next to me in our stage-box looking very pretty in her pale blue dress. And then from the orchestra pit, a great black hole full of little lights, there suddenly rose the dim figure of my father, light and supple, to be greeted with a burst of applause. He reached the conductor's desk in a single bound, bowed to the audience turned round and quietly proceeded to break his conductor's baton. I held my breath . . . but he simply found it inconveniently long! Then there was Monsieur Ansermet with his black beard on his white shirt-front. At the interval there were the shining, slippery floors, men in tail-coats, scented women and the Geneva police in their full dress-uniform – two-cornered hat, epaulettes, shoulder-knots, shoulder-belts and white gloves . . . the glittering chandeliers were reflected a myriad times in the foyer's huge mirrors . . . And I shall never forget the appearance in our box of the magnificent white lady who had sung the Russian national anthem 'God save the Tsar' on the stage at the beginning of the evening. Felia Litvinne had been one of the glories of the Imperial Opera in St. Petersburg and it was she who now turned to me and, pressing me against her ample bosom, whispered in Russian 'You know, little Theodore, before you were born, I sang with your grandfather, big Theodore'. I can still smell the strange vanilla-like scent of her make-up. I was slightly intimidated but then Uncle Serge appeared in front of the curtain, bowing and holding the pretty ballerinas by the hand . . . What a host of emotions and new impressions that evening brought! and what a miraculous thing is the small human being's faculty of absorption, when confronted for the first time with a wonderful dream world which suddenly becomes real and immediately impresses itself for ever on his memory!

Our family circle at Morges was enriched by the presence of dear old Bertha Essert, a German national whom my father had been able to regain in spite of the war. She had been in his parents' household before he was born and had been the faithful *niania* of his youth. Having done all she could to spoil Igor and his brothers, she did just the same for Igor's children. What in fact is a *niania*? Neither a diploma, nor a function – not even that of overseer, though that may enter into it, I should say rather that it is an acquired status. There was not a single Russian family with any pretention to comfortable means that had not its *niania*, an indispensable moral support to the family and a kind of surrogate to the grandmothers, arousing no jealousy because she was not taking anybody else's place. On the contrary, a *niania* completed the traditional Russian family, rounding it off, as it were. A *niania* obtained her family rights in exactly the same way as city rights used to be obtained, by long devotion to the common cause. She knew that she would end her days respected and loved by one, two, even three generations. There have even been *nianias* who have become famous, like Pushkin's, whom the poet celebrated in unforgettable lines. Well, dear good Bertha was our *niania* as she had been my father's, and we all loved her as though she were a real granny. She died suddenly one fine spring afternoon in 1917. There was a great stir in the house followed by a sudden silence. Everybody lowered their voices and walked about on tiptoe, while strange men went up and down the stairs. For the first time I saw my mother and father in tears and their close friends being strangely gentle and protective towards them . . . A Lutheran pastor in a long black coat came, and I was struck by the melancholy deference with which my father treated him . . . It was in fact the first time that I found myself face to face with the mysterious reality of death, though not long before I had been made at least remotely aware of its existence. Sophie Velsovksy – 'Baba Sonia' – who had been *niania* to my mother and her sister, had also died, but that was far away in Russia, with the Belyankins. I was just coming in from school and found mamma in tears and papa offering her all the consolation his tender affection could devise. 'Baba Sonia is dead, we shall never see her again . . .' Dear Baba Sonia, so intimately linked to all our memories up to 1914 . . .

The Villa Rogivue became a very sad place, until Mina Svitalski came to us as governess and was not long in becoming our new *niania* – the tender-hearted unforgettable 'Madubo', a name my brother gave her as soon as he saw her and adopted by all of us and our friends. She was to stay the rest of her life with one or other of us, and having brought all four of us up was to nanny Ludmila's little daughter Catherine and Soulima's son John. After she had spent more than forty years with the Stravinsky family it fell to my lot to be present at her death.

With Bertha gone my parents felt the need of a change of scene. In the traditional Russian fashion the whole household moved for the summer of 1917 into the mountains, to Les Diablerets in the Vaud Alps. Leading the procession went the piano; then came suitcases and packages; our dog Mouche and a complete farmyard of animals in wicker cages; followed by the cook, the housemaid, the governess, Madubo, papa, mamma and us four children. We all stayed at a chalet called Les Fougères owned by a retired joiner, an excellent man who allowed 'the Russian gentleman, an eccentric' to take possession of what had been his workshop. On the astonished walls of this unusual work-room there immediately appeared photographs of the extraordinary 'sandwich-men' that Picasso had designed for *Parade*, the ballet by Erik Satie and Jean Cocteau that Diaghilev had just given in Rome. Stravinsky worked that whole summer at the joiner's workbench on the last scene of *Les Noces*.

Through this workshop window I one day caught sight of a figure that I did not know – a man with a pale, flat, round, smooth face, with large spectacles, who was talking excitedly with my father. Then they played cards in an arbour at the bottom of the garden; and when the man, in his loose *Lodenmantel* had been seen off at the village station, Father came back and told us 'He was furious because he kept on losing!' We, on the other hand, were always being told that one must never be angry when one was beaten at a game! The man who lost at cards that afternoon was André Gide. Many years later there would be a Stravinsky-Gide collaboration in *Persephone*; but although this was the occasion of many meetings, two such fundamentally different personalities could never really become close to each other.

Another visit was that of Jacques Copeau, who brought his daughter Mayenne, a girl of about our age with beautiful long fair hair that made a great impression on me . . .

It was an unusually fine summer, and Father was often tempted to join us when we made excursions. I can remember returning to Les Fougères one day after spending a long afternoon picking raspberries in the woods, each of us delightedly carrying his bucket of light, sweet-smelling little fruit, and hearing my parents say 'What a really marvellous day!' At that moment a telegraph-boy arrived on a bicycle. Father read the telegram and handed it to Mother. 'Uncle Gouri is dead', she said. 'A long, long way away', said my father slowly, 'on the Rumanian front'. He took my mother's hand and we went silently into the house. The blood relationship between Igor and Catherine Stravinsky, who were first cousins, gave them an extraordinary unity in the face of family griefs and family joys.

Back at Morges our parents were faced with an unexpected problem. The Villa Rogivue, which had been our home since May 1915, just been sold by the owner, and we therefore had to move again, and without delay. Fortunately they found a delightful roomy apartment a few yards away in the handsome XVIIIth century dwelling called 'Maison Bornand', Place St. Louis. And so we children had to say good-bye to the lovely big garden which had been the scene of our games for more than two years.

Igor and Catherine found it difficult to reconcile themselves to being deprived of all contacts with their own country; after the October Revolution they had to make up their minds to the fact that this separation was final. That fact, and the very natural sense of homesickness that it brought, may well explain Stravinsky's passionate enthusiasm at his period for Russian folk-poetry and his loving examination and use of its inexhaustible riches. This folklore was to be a real speciality of his and *Pribautki*, *Berceuses du chat*, *Quatre Chants Russes*, *Les Noces* and *Renard* – all vocal works – constitute a kind of creative monopoly in this field.

Here something must be said of my father's collaboration with C.F.Ramuz. What Stravinsky wanted was not so much a translation of his texts, as a French version that did not betray his own original Russian prosody. It needed the sensibility and intuition of a poet like Ramuz, tuned to the same wave-length (personal as well as aesthetic) as Stravinsky's, to accomplish a sort of miracle and achieve success in a plan that must have seemed mad to them – for the author of the French version did not know a word of Russian! In fact this collaboration was as satisfying to both parties as it is possible to imagine. Anyone who doubts this has only to turn to the passage in Stravinsky's *Chroniques de ma vie* where he speaks of this collaboration and to the admirable passages in Ramuz's own *Souvenirs sur Igor Stravinsky*.

Stravinsky, like Ramuz, always distrusted theories. Both were attached to the concrete and their reflections on artistic matters never took on the character of dissertations. The two friends met almost daily, and when we were not at school we used to like to go down to the station early in the morning to meet Monsieur Ramuz, who only returned to Lausanne by the last train in the evening.

The chief fruit of the Stravinsky-Ramuz collaboration was *L'Histoire du Soldat* (*The Soldier's Tale*). In this case the original text is by Ramuz himself, based on a theme taken from a Russian folk-story that Stravinsky told him. The setting of the story was changed to an imaginary Vaud. Here I should like to add a small parenthesis. My father liked to tell how one night in 1918, when he was working on *L'Histoire du Soldat*, he dreamed of a handsome gypsy-woman sitting at the door of her caravan, suckling her child and at the same time playing a tango on the violin. 'This is the only time,' Igor Stravinsky used to say, 'that I ever managed to remember clearly a musical phrase heard in a dream and to write it down complete. Musical dreams generally disperse into thin air when the dreamer wakes.' The Gypsy's theme became the tango in *L'Histoire du Soldat*. According to the advertisements the play is to be 'read, played and danced'. Economy was the rule, owing to the material difficulties of the times, and the cast consists of three actor-dancers, one reader and seven musicians. It was these conditions that prompted the composer to create a new musical language, deliberately austere in character.

The four friends used to meet in our house – Stravinsky, Ramuz, Ansermet and René Auberjonois, who was to do the sets and costumes. At mealtimes Father's moods provided a reliable barometer of the climate in which these meetings took place. This was sometimes rough, and the weather chart veered between 'fine', 'changeable' and 'stormy' . . . but all the preparatory work took place in an atmosphere of enthusiasm. The first performance was at Lausanne on 29 September 1918, and, as my father was to write later, it gave him more satisfaction than the performance of any other stage work of his.

I felt enormously proud and happy looking at my schoolfriends sitting in their best clothes in the neighbouring box with their parents. Among all my memories of the performance I must mention Elie Gagnebin's unforgettable reading of the Narrator's part, a masterpiece of acting that delighted us all. His long friendship with all our family was to date from *The Soldier's Tale*. At the end of September 1918 everyone was making optimistic plans for touring with the new work, but in fact the first performance was to remain for years the only performance the work ever had. Authors, actors and musicians all succumbed to the terrible epidemic which raged throughout Europe under the name of 'Spanish influenza'.

Everyone had to take to their beds, and I can still see Father buried under piles of blankets, his teeth chattering, a big beret pulled down over his eyes and in a very bad temper, while my mother staggered round in her dressing-gown handing out medicines, infusions and linctuses to the whole family. The planned tour was postponed indefinitely and it was only later, in different surroundings and circumstances, that the work was to have its great success.

Although *The Soldier's Tale* was unquestionably one of Stravinsky's chief works and Diaghilev was certainly one of my father's first admirers, this pioneer, this innovator with his fine nose for quality turned up his nose at the new work! It had not been produced under his aegis. Was the favourite colt in fact about to escape from the Diaghilev stables?

We are now coming to the last year of our life at Morges. The war is over and my father's visits to Paris have become more and more frequent. In my memories this whole period is overshadowed by the chief work that engaged Stravinsky – *Pulcinella*. He had brought back from one of his journey's a collection of unpublished works and unfinished fragments of Pergolesi's, things that Diaghilev had picked up in different European libraries. They were to provide the composer with the musical substance for a new ballet. It was at this time that Pablo Picasso, who was already a famous artist, became a household name with the Stravinsky family. He had been a friend of my father's for some years, but it was only when he undertook the sets and costumes for the ballet *Pulcinella* that a closer bond was established between painter and musician. The confrontation of three such personalities as Diaghilev, Stravinsky and Picasso could not fail to produce sparks enough to illumine the whole firmament. But a mutual confidence, born of a mutual admiration, united the three great men, overcoming all obstacles, and the result of their collaboration was one of the greatest successes achieved by the Ballets Russes. Picasso became a family figure to us, and this familiarity took on a concrete form in the series of drawings, gouaches and painting that he presented to my parents. My mother gave the place of honour on our walls to the famous full-face pencil portrait of the composer, with the dedication 'To Stravinsky from his friend Picasso'.

However far back I pursue my childhood memories, I can find no break in my wish to be a painter 'when I'm grown up'. Contact with Picasso's work, and soon after that with the artist himself, was to have the effect of a catalyst on me. I met with nothing but encouragement from my parents, both of whom were deeply sensitive to the visual arts, or from their painter friends and my path was thus clear. The same was soon to be true of my brother Soulima, who had wanted to be a pianist from his earliest youth. He had unquestionable talent, as my father was delighted to observe, and very soon Igor Stravinsky's own son was to include all his father's piano works in the repertory which he played all over the world. But we must not anticipate the future . . . except, perhaps, to observe, in passing that the great-grandson of Feodor Ignatievich Stravinsky, John, Igor's grandson and Soulima's son seems to be showing a real vocation for the stage . . .

But we must return to Morges and the year 1920. The international situation after the war provided a new field of activity in which a comparatively young artist such as my father could make a brilliant career. Morges, to which wartime conditions had confined our family life, was a charming little town, but he could no longer make it his home. After considering Rome as a possibility for some time, my parents decided to transfer their household goods to Paris. But as if the Stravinsky's themselves were not numerous enough, they had now been joined by my uncle Belyankin's family, which had somehow managed to escape from Russia and had joined us at Morges. My mother and my aunt, who were very close to each other, were at last united again, and we children rediscovered our cousins, a boy and a girl. So once again Father set out at the head of a complete tribe, like any patriarch – only it was my uncle who had the beard – on the journey from Morges to Paris and a new life.

The preparations for the move were no small matter, as may be imagined. Father thought of everything and took everything in hand, while Mother and Madubo attended to the practical details, and we children went round saying good-bye to school-friends and schoolmasters.

Everything is upside down in the Maison Bornand. Everywhere there are suitcases, trunks, packing-cases, straw, draughts, removal men and glasses of wine. The chairs have been packed, so we sat on packing-cases to chat with all the friends who came round to say good-bye. 'Well, Ramuz', I heard Father saying 'you're not coming with us?' 'Really, Stravinsky how could I? . . . Paris is the devil of a way away . . . and I'm no globetrotter like you' – This was a line that

Ramuz was fond of taking.

In the perspective of the years it seems clear, as I wrote at the beginning of this album, that the division of my father's life into three periods is not too arbitrary and that the first of these ended precisely at this time – early summer 1920, when Switzerland and Morges are to be left.

At last the great day for our departure arrived. There were more than a dozen of us, counting grown-ups and children, and we spread ourselves over I don't know how many compartments. We stopped at Geneva, from where we were to take the night train to Paris a few hours later. The Ansermets came to the station, loaded with little presents, and other friends came too to wave us good-bye. Meanwhile we ate sandwiches at the station buffet and the little ones were given glasses of grenadine. But on that occasion my father counted me among the grown-ups and with a serious face poured out my first *real glass of beer*. To this day I can see him doing it – and perhaps that should count as one of the last memories of my youth, reminding me irresistibly of my very earliest childhood. And once again in our family annals there is a great counting and recounting of parcels and suitcases on a railway platform; but one particular case is never lost sight of, one that is heavy in more senses than one and precious above all others – the one containing Igor Stravinsky's already numerous manuscripts.

Théodore Stravinsky

Avertissement

On peut diviser, sans trop d'arbitraire me semble-t-il, la vie de mon père Igor Strawinsky en trois parties distinctes.

La première qui va jusqu'à 1920 et constitue le thème de cet album pourrait être intitulée 'de Russie en Occident'.

La deuxième correspondrait à la vie du compositeur, avec sa famille, en France de 1920 à 1939.

Enfin la troisième, de 1939 à sa mort en 1971, recouvrirait les années que mon père vécut aux Etats-Unis.

C'est exclusivement la première partie de cette longue existence que les courts récits qui suivent cherchent à évoquer plutôt qu'à raconter. Gravitant autour d'un noyau de souvenirs d'enfance, choses vues, vécues, conservées comme telles dans ma mémoire et qui sont étayées par ce que je tiens directement de mes parents concernant les miens, ils accompagnent un choix de photographies de famille, pour la plupart inédites et qui me viennent de ma mère. L'ensemble – texte et photos – se présente ainsi comme une succession de flashes éclairant la vie familiale de mon père jusqu'en 1920 et recouvrant par conséquent la période de mon enfance. Quoi d'étonnant dès lors que la musique ne tienne dans ces pages qu'une place marginale? Les oeuvres paternelles n'y seront citées qu'à titre de points de repère chronologiques.

Enfin, cinq photographies, prises par ma femme à Evian fin août 1970, soit quelques mois seulement avant la mort de mon père, apporteront à cet 'Album de Famille' un bouleversant épilogue.

Th. S.

Igor et Catherine Strawinsky, mes parents, au coeur de mes souvenirs d'enfance

Feodor Ignatevitch et Anna Kyrillovna, les parents d'Igor Stawinsky, faisaient, à la fin du siècle dernier, partie intégrante du milieu musical de Saint-Petersbourg, alors capitale de la Russie.

Feodor Ignatevitch Strawinsky (Théodore, fils d'Ignace), né en 1843, descendait d'une vieille famille d'origine polonaise. Il fit carrière comme basse-chantante au Théâtre-Marie, l'Opéra impérial. Le registre très étendu de sa voix chaude et prenante et ses dons exceptionnels d'acteur lui valurent très vite une grande renommée. Esprit ouvert, il s'appliqua à débarrasser la vénérable vieille scène petersbourgeoise des désuètes routines qui l'empoussiéraient et introduisit, en novateur, un style de jeu réaliste et vivant. Théodore Strawinsky, mon grand-père, marquera d'une forte empreinte personnelle le théâtre lyrique russe de son époque. Fin lettré, il se constituera une importante bibliothèque. Son épouse, Anna Kyrillovna (Anne, fille de Cyrille), née Kholodowsky, était dotée, elle, d'une jolie voix de mezzo-soprano mais n'en fit pas carrière, se contentant de chanter pour son seul plaisir; elle était bonne musicienne. Son fils Igor ne dira-t-il pas un jour: 'C'est d'elle que j'ai reçu le don précieux de déchiffrer les partitions d'orchestre.'

Couple exemplaire, mais peut-être parents trop exigeants, Théodore et Anna Strawinsky connurent, semble-t-il, pas mal de difficultés dans l'éducation des quatre turbulents garçons qu'étaient leurs fils Roman, Youri, Igor et Gouri.

De cordiales relations de famille liaient ceux-ci à leurs nombreux cousins Yellatchitch et à leurs tout aussi nombreuses cousines Nossenko. Chaque été on se retrouvait joyeusement dans les propriétés rurales des uns ou des autres.

C'est à Saint-Petersbourg, la belle capitale des Tzars à l'architecture palladienne, qu'Igor et ses frères passent leur enfance et leur adolescence. Igor y fera ses études de droit, pour se plier aux exigences raisonnables de ses parents; de musique, pour satisfaire à celles impérieuses de son unique penchant. C'est aussi à Saint-Petersbourg qu'Igor Feodorovitch Strawinsky et Ekaterina Gavrilovna Nossenko (Catherine, fille de Gabriel) sa cousine, unissent leurs destinées le 24 janvier 1906, qu'ils passent les trois premières années de leur mariage et que voient le jour leurs deux premiers enfants, Théodore et Ludmila, 1907-1908.

1910. C'est l'hiver, un jeune homme de 27 ans, penché vers le petit garçon pâlot de 3 ans à peine que j'étais, scande joyeusement en plaisantant et en chantant: '*Vivement, vivement un boc de bière!*' pour lui faire avaler, sur prescription médicale, une pleine cuillerée de sang de boeuf. Le petit jeu se répétera à chaque repas et l'horrible chose passera . . . en musique! Déjà paternel, Igor avait pour son premier-né Théodore de touchantes prévenances. Voilà le plus ancien souvenir que ma mémoire, aujourd'hui sexagénaire, ait retenu d'Igor Strawinsky, mon père.

Avant cela aucun souvenir mais cette petite histoire cocasse que je tiens de mon père lui-même: lorsque je naquis, ma mère ne pouvant m'allaiter, il fallut en hâte trouver une nourrice. On consulta les annonces, Igor se rendit dans une agence de placement et là lui furent présentées, alignées, plusieurs jeunes personnes tous seins découverts et, tour à tour, chacune de gicler quelques gouttes de son précieux breuvage dans un petit gobelet que l'on tendait au jeune père prié d'apprécier. J'ignore quel fut son critère mais l'élue donna, paraît-il, toute satisfaction . . .

Le climat de la grande ville nordique où l'hiver avec ses rigueurs s'attarde indéfiniment alors que l'été avec ses langoureuses nuits blanches passe comme un rêve, n'était pas fait pour la santé délicate de ma mère. Très vite mon père devait s'en préoccuper. L'appartement petersbourgeois de la Perspective des Anglais n'abritera plus longtemps le foyer du jeune couple. Dès 1910 mes parents décident d'abandonner les rives de la Neva. A partir de cette époque mon père n'y reviendra que seul et n'y fera que de brefs séjours pour son travail. Quant à la famille qui ira s'accroissant – il y a déjà et il y aura toujours des nianias, des gouvernantes, des oncles, des tantes, des grand'mères – elle mènera désormais et jusqu'à la guerre de 1914 une existence constamment itinérante. Igor et Catherine venaient de construire à Oustiloug, en Volhynie, à l'extrême sud-ouest de la Russie, sur des terres appartenant à ma mère et à sa soeur Ludmila, une demeure rurale et estivale qui chaque été abritera notre famille jusqu'à l'automne 1913 et chaque année, à la mauvaise saison, la maisonnée au complet se transportera sous des cieux plus cléments, en Europe occidentale: en Suisse ou sur la Riviera française. Ainsi, de 1909 à 1914, ma prime enfance connut-elle un régime de perpétuel va-et-vient. Saint-Petersbourg–Oustiloug, Oustiloug–La Baule, Clarens, Beaulieu, Oustiloug, Clarens . . .

Mais arrêtons-nous quelque peu à Oustiloug où se situent les souvenirs les plus exquis de mes premières années. Choses et évènements commencent alors à se marquer de plus en plus nettement dans ma mémoire. Les étés d'Oustiloug me ravissaient. Ils inondent rétrospectivement mon enfance d'une lumière heureuse.

Les arbres nouvellement plantés donnaient autour de la maison une petite ombre fraîche et légère. Une simple palissade en bois nous séparait de nos cousins; la sœur de ma mère avait épousé un officier de marine, Grégoire Beliankine, elle lui donna deux enfants, une fille et un garçon, Ira et Gania. Une très étroite affection unira toujours ma mère et ma tante, ce sera le lien vivant entre nos familles. Les deux ménages avaient construit deux maisons voisines. Si la nôtre était sobre, celle des Beliankine, flanquée d'une tour carrée et d'un péristyle semi-circulaire inachevé (il devait toujours le rester!), me paraissait le summum de la splendeur . . . et à l'arrière cet endroit mystérieux, cet enclos grillagé où quatre énormes chiens St Bernard avaient toujours l'air d'attendre quelque chose . . . Et que dire de la pétaradante et fascinante Dedion-Bouton de mon oncle aux énormes phares de laiton? Je ressentais comme une humiliation que mes parents n'en eussent pas une eux aussi. Avec quelles délices je manipulais l'énorme poire en caoutchouc de la trompette qui cassait les oreilles des grandes personnes toujours si délicates! Tandis que je triomphais, hissé aux côtés de mon oncle sur le siège en molesquine, la course en plein vent autour de la pelouse me paraissait folle . . . En revanche devant la maison paternelle et sous les fenêtres de mon père la consigne était au silence. Son cabinet de travail, grande pièce carrée où j'aimais à me glisser est aujourd'hui encore, jusque dans ses moindres détails, gravé dans ma mémoire. Les murs couverts d'images, le haut pupitre, le bureau Empire aux grands tiroirs, plumes et crayons, règles et gommes, encres multicolores dans de petits flacons de cristal, grattoirs de tous calibres et de différentes formes, presse-papiers japonais . . . que d'objets d'autant plus attirants qu'on ne devait jamais y toucher! C'est en ce haut-lieu où tout me paraissait merveilleux que je fis un jour, par le truchement d'une gravure, la connaissance d'Alexandre Pouchkine. Devant le portrait du poète mon père m'expliqua qui était ce monsieur et ce qu'était un écrivain. Pouchkine, en russe, veut dire *du canon*. C'est cela qui me fit le plus d'impression! Sur le grand piano à queue où il avait récemment composé *Feu d'Artifice* pour le mariage de la fille de Rimsky-Korsakov, mon père avait toujours une partition

en travail. Le vieux maître n'avait-il pas, un jour, répondu à son jeune élève qui lui demandait s'il faisait bien de composer au piano: 'Les uns composent au piano, les autres sans piano. Eh! bien, vous, vous composerez au piano.' Mû par un besoin impérieux de contact direct avec la matière sonore, Strawinsky, on le sait, composera toute sa vie au piano.

A Oustiloug, éloigné de tout centre intellectuel, la famille, il est vrai déjà fort nombreuse, vivait forcément repliée sur elle-même. Je ne me souviens que d'un seul visage nouveau, celui de Stéphane Mitoussov, grand ami de mon père qui avait élaboré avec lui le livret du *Rossignol*. A Oustiloug Strawinsky mettra le point final à la partition de l'*Oiseau de Feu* au printemps 1910. Oustiloug, de l'aveu même du compositeur, lui offrait la retraite idéale pour se livrer à la composition.

Sur ces terres, au cœur d'une contrée essentiellement rurale, vivaient beaucoup de Juifs, tous de condition très modeste. Au temps de la récolte on les voyait camper dans les vergers alentour sous de grandes tentes. Un jour une belle et souriante Raïssa vient sonner à la porte. Je vois encore ma mère lui ouvrir et moi de me trouver, ô stupeur! nez à nez avec les becs ouverts de deux poulets aux yeux hagards, tenus liés ensemble par les pattes; elle venait vendre sa volaille. Ma surprise fut à son comble lorsque, levant la tête, je vis l'étrange coiffure de la jeune femme, sorte de bonnet sur lequel étaient peints des cheveux roux. Je n'eus de cesse qu'on me dise . . . et mon père m'expliqua que les femmes juives, du moins dans cette région, se rasaient la tête pour le jour de leurs noces et que celles qui ne pouvaient s'offrir une véritable perruque se contentaient de peindre soigneusement, sur un bonnet de toile, de faux cheveux avec raie au milieu.

Au déclin de la belle saison, les préparatifs de départ déclenchent chaque année au sein de la famille un branle-bas général. Parents, grand'mères, nianias et gouvernantes bouclent les valises, ferment les malles, sanglent les panières japonaises sans oublier les mémorables cartons à chapeaux — inconnus des enfants d'aujourd'hui — que la *belle époque* avait démesurément amplifiés. C'est alors qu'Igor rassemble tout son monde. Un silence. L'ancestrale coutume russe exige que lorsque l'on quitte en famille un lieu, si l'on veut y revenir, il faut s'asseoir au moment du départ, tous ensemble — *prissest'* — se recueillir quelques secondes et se signer en se relevant. Cette observance était universellement respectée dans la Russie d'alors et mes parents aimaient à s'y conformer. Nous les petits, malgré notre agitation, ressentions ces courts instants comme quelque chose de très solennel … mais de très long !

Déjà sur le perron s'entassent coffres et valises. On prend place dans les voitures. Les chevaux piaffent, hennissent. Un coup de fouet, signal du départ et . . . au revoir Oustiloug, jusqu'à l'an prochain ! Après plusieurs heures de cahots Vladimir-Volhynsk, puis Kovel le soir. Dans le silence nocturne, sous le ciel étoilé, la résonnance de nos pas sur les trottoirs en bois de la petite ville : j'ai un peu peur, mais la main de mon père, tenant la mienne, me rassure. A l'hôtel notre mère saupoudre soigneusement nos draps d'un produit jaune 'pour chasser les puces'; cela faisait partie de nos divertissements de voyage. Le lendemain la petite gare dans la piquante fraîcheur matinale, le train poussif jusqu'à Varsovie. Là, en attendant l'express de Berlin, goûter au buffet de la gare, ce buffet au milieu duquel trônait, lançant ses jets de vapeur, un immense samovar chrômé en forme de locomotive ; il magnétisait mes regards. Sur le quai père et mère comptent et recomptent les bagages tandis que tout notre monde se répartit dans les compartiments feutrés de l'express international au personnel galonné.

Vingt-quatre heures à Berlin. Cette journée dans la capitale allemande était toujours merveilleusement marquée par une visite au *Tiergarten* et une autre, non moins merveilleuse, au rayon 'jouets' d'un grand magasin. C'est là qu'une fois, après un long essayage, on m'acheta, à ma grande fierté, mon premier costume marin. Mon père, enfreignant la réglementation d'hygiène, essaya tour à tour plusieurs sifflets, à la grande confusion de ma mère mais à ma joie – bien que je fusse un peu gêné car les vendeuses nous regardaient – et s'arrêta sur le plus strident qu'il épingla, tel une décoration, sur mon nouveau costume. Ce jour-là il se fit subitement dans le magasin un grand mouvement. Dehors, un klaxon au timbre particulier avait retenti. Tout le monde de se précipiter vers portes et fenêtres et mon père de me hisser sur ses épaules pour que, moi aussi, je visse passer, dans une grande automobile blanche découverte, un monsieur très sérieux, saluant de la main : le Kaiser.

La gloire montante du très jeune compositeur qu'était alors Igor Strawinsky faisait déjà accourir à la gare, pour le saluer, la direction *in corpore* de l'Edition Russe de Musique qui avait son siège à Berlin et c'était, pour ses enfants, la distribution assurée de sucreries berlinoises.

Etape Paris. Nuit à l'Hôtel d'Egypte, rue des Pyramides. Trônant sur la haute cheminée la solennelle pendule en marbre noir au cadran doré, flanquée de deux sphynx en laiton, avait un tic-tac sonore qui finit par avoir raison de mon excitation de petit voyageur et je m'endormis enfin, ô privilège ! dans le lit de mes parents.

Et de nouveau le train. Enfin La Baule ! Après l'interminable voyage, à peine arrivés au but, mon père se donne la joie d'amener sur l'heure son fils vers l'immense océan et de lui en faire goûter, pour la première fois, l'eau salée. Cousin, cousine et petite soeur n'eurent pas l'avantage de cette initiation, ils étaient restés avec les grandes personnes qui ouvraient les valises. Sur la plage, j'entends encore le refrain du marchand de gauffres : 'Arrivez papas, arrivez mamans, faites plaisir à vos enfants !' La demeure louée pour la fin de l'été était un chalet couleur chocolat, situé au milieu des pins. C'est là que mon père composera ses *Deux Poèmes de Verlaine* pour baryton et piano dédiés à son frère Gouri, chanteur comme leur père. Notre oncle était alors à La Baule avec nous. Après quelques semaines la famille gagne la Suisse et le 23 septembre 1910, à Lausanne, ma mère donne le jour à son troisième enfant, notre frère Sviatoslav-Soulima.

L'hiver se passera à Beaulieu-sur-Mer. Un appartement au premier étage ; au rez-de-chaussée, quelle aubaine ! une confiserie : on mange des violettes et du mimosa au sucre. Et tandis que mon père, travaillant à *Petrouchka*, compose les scènes de liesse populaire de la Semaine Grasse – lesquelles se déroulent, on le sait, à Saint-Petersbourg sur le fond d'une nordique pénombre hivernale – sous ses fenêtres, par un brillant soleil méditerranéen, passent et repassent les masques du Carnaval de Beaulieu. Le soir mon père entraîne mère et tantes au cortège et le lendemain ma soeur et moi avec cousin et cousine, à quatre pattes, ramassons dans tous les coins de l'appartement des confettis aux mille couleurs.

Toujours à Beaulieu, devant moi deux énormes et rutilantes chasubles d'or, des nuées d'encens emplissant la salle à manger, une grande bassine de cuivre pleine d'eau, beaucoup de chants et dans mes mains un gros cierge allumé. Tout me paraît si beau ! C'est le baptême de notre petit frère. Père et mère ont toujours eu le plus grand respect pour les choses sacrées, les rites et les traditions de l'Eglise Orthodoxe. Avec les années la foi s'enracinera de plus en plus en eux et mon père lui-même que les circonstances de la vie écarteront plus tard de la pratique religieuse conservera néanmoins, au plus profond de son être, une foi inaltérée.

Encore Beaulieu. Bientôt, le printemps touchant à sa fin, mon père fait un bref séjour à Rome où il termine *Petrouchka* puis rejoint la famille qui va reprendre le chemin de la Russie pour y retrouver à Oustiloug le bel été d'Ukraine avec ses fruits savoureux, ses fraises blanches au parfum d'ananas. Un petit enfant de plus . . . une nurse de plus!

Strawinsky ébauche en ces jours-là une cantate pour chœur d'hommes et orchestre: *Le Roi des Etoiles* dédié à Claude Debussy et compose un diptyque vocal: *Deux Poèmes de Balmont, le Myosotis* et *le Pigeon* respectivement dédiés à sa mère et à sa belle-sœur Ludmila Beliankine, mais surtout, reprenant une idée qui le hantait déjà bien avant *Petrouchka*, il met en chantier *Le Sacre du Printemps*.

Les premiers frimas de l'automne vont de nouveau chasser tout notre monde, cette fois vers les rives du Léman, en Suisse, à Clarens, Pension les Tilleuls.

A ses multiples installations passagères mon père sut toujours conférer un aspect quasi-définitif et s'y réserver l'isolement indispensable pour la création. Toute sa vie, partout, il suscitera autour de lui son climat propre. Les plus anonymes des chambres d'hôtel reçoivent son cachet personnel, je dirais presque sa signature. Les murs alors révèlent tout ce qui le passionne au moment même, du plus noble antique à l'image d'Epinal. Mais en ces années-là ce sont les estampes japonaises qui ont la place d'honneur, art que l'élite européenne découvrait, redécouvrait avec ferveur; et Strawinsky compose les *Trois Poésies de la Lyrique Japonaise* pour voix aiguë et piano: *Akahito* dédié à Maurice Delage, *Mazatsumi* à Florent Schmitt, et *Tsaraiuki* à Maurice Ravel.

Accoudé au fer forgé du balcon, devant nos fenêtres (Hôtel du Châtelard), je vois encore aux côtés de mon père un petit monsieur impeccable, aux yeux de braise, aux gros sourcils touffus et à la belle chevelure légèrement argentée. Je les entends encore tous deux sifflant cinq, dix, quinze fois une courte phrase musicale aux merles du jardin, lesquels finirent, à ma joie d'enfant, par la leur renvoyer. Le petit monsieur n'était autre que Maurice Ravel.

Leur goût commun pour l'art japonais et les recherches esthétiques de Ravel et de Strawinsky, pour autant qu'elles s'apparentaient à ce moment-là, alimentaient leur amitié. Les deux musiciens vécurent quelques semaines en voisins (printemps 1913) se voyant quotidiennement. Seule la voie ferrée séparait l'Hôtel des Crêtes où résidait le compositeur français, de l'Hôtel du Châtelard (aujourd'hui démoli) où vivaient le compositeur russe avec sa famille. Si celui-ci était venu chercher à Clarens un climat qui convînt à la santé de sa jeune femme, Ravel, lui, accompagné de sa mère, retrouvait dans la région le berceau de sa famille. Ces lieux seraient-ils prédestinés pour accueillir les musiciens? Mendelssohn y séjourne longuement, Tchaikowsky y compose *la Pucelle d'Orléans* et de nos jours Paul Hindemith y passe les dernières années de sa vie.

Strawinsky, lui, achève à l'Hôtel de Châtelard *Le Sacre du Printemps*.

Ici arrêtons-nous. N'y a-t-il pas lieu de s'émerveiller de la stupéfiante vitalité créatrice dont fait preuve le jeune musicien de trente ans? Ne réalise-t-il pas en trois ans (1910–1913) les trois chefs d'œuvre qui vont le placer au faîte de la renommée? *L'Oiseau de Feu, Petrouchka, Le Sacre du Printemps*. Et cela, nous l'avons vu, en assumant pleinement, en vrai patriarche, les charges d'une famille qui vit dans une atmosphère de perpétuelle transhumance. Et il trouve encore le temps d'y ajouter de multiples déplacements personnels; ne va-t-il pas à tout moment rejoindre Diaghilev et sa troupe à Paris, à Rome, à Bayreuth . . .? La fracassante Première du *Sacre* eut lieu, on le sait, le 29 mai 1913 au Théâtre des Champs-Elysées à Paris. Quelques jours après, une fièvre typhoïde contractée et soignée dans la capitale française semble vouloir prendre une tournure dramatique, elle alarme et fait trembler parents et amis du compositeur.

L'été se passe de nouveau, comme toujours, en famille à Oustiloug. Le convalescent y compose 'pour se divertir' *Souvenirs de mon enfance*, trois petites pièces pour chant et piano qu'il dédie à ses trois enfants, Théodore, Ludmila, Sviatoslav-Soulima. Pièces dont vingt ans plus tard il fera une transcription pour petit ensemble instrumental.

En automne, retour à Clarens. Mais qui donc pouvait se douter que la Russie cette fois-ci était quittée pour toujours et Oustiloug perdu à jamais?

Le 15 janvier 1914 notre sœur Milène, quatrième et dernier enfant de nos parents, voit le jour à Lausanne. Notre mère, épuisée par ses couches, est envoyée pour un séjour prolongé en montagne, à Leysin, où son mari l'accompagne faisant preuve de cette anxiété et de cette sollicitude qui le caractériseront toujours dès qu'il s'agira de la santé des siens. C'est à Leysin que devait se sceller entre mes parents et Jean Cocteau une amitié véritable ; véritable car, malgré de nombreux tiraillements, agacements et même quelques éclipses, elle ne se démentit jamais et ne pouvait manquer d'aboutir un jour à une étroite collaboration autour d'une grande oeuvre scénique. Ce sera le cas, en 1926, avec *Oedipus Rex*.

Si nos parents décidèrent en 1914 de ne pas retourner pour l'été, selon la coutume établie, en Russie mais de rester à l'altitude en Suisse, ils étaient loin de soupçonner les conséquences déterminantes pour le reste de leur vie de cette décision uniquement dictée par un souci passager de santé. En effet, après Leysin et tandis que toute la famille s'était transportée dans la petite station estivale de Salvan en Valais, pension Bel-Air, éclata la Première Guerre Mondiale. N'étant pas mobilisable mon père n'était pas tenu de rentrer dans son pays. Il ne reverra le sol natal qu'après son quatre-vingtième anniversaire . . . quarante huit ans plus tard !

Le 26 mai avait enfin eu lieu à Paris la Première du *Rossignol*, oeuvre commencée déjà à Saint-Petersbourg en 1908 et longtemps restée inachevée. A Salvan ce seront les maquettes de cet opéra, offertes par leur auteur Alexandre Benois à son ami Igor Strawinsky, qui vont orner la pièce où travaillera mon père. Il y composera *Pribaoutki* en pensant à la voix de son frère Gouri et *Trois Pièces pour Quatuor à Cordes*.

C'est là qu'un jour l'air sombre et préoccupé de mes parents me fit comprendre qu'il se passait quelque chose de très grave. 'On dit que ce sera la guerre' m'expliqua, bouleversée, ma grand'mère qui était alors avec nous. Peu de jours après c'était, pour l'armée suisse neutre, la mobilisation générale et des exercices de tir quotidiens eurent lieu dans le pré en face de notre pension. Mes petits camarades et moi eûmes tôt fait d'inventer un jeu avec les douilles vides que fièrement nous glânions. Aux heures des repas, à la table d'hôte, on voyait mon père user de toutes sortes de petites ruses pour échapper aux envahissantes théories d'une *célèbre* et redoutable dame théosophe . . . et à nous, nous enjoindre de ne pas accepter les exquis pains d'épices à la confiture qu'elle voulait sans cesse nous offrir !

L'automne venu on redescend à Clarens, cette fois non plus à l'hôtel mais dans une villa sous-louée à Ernest Ansermet. On sait les liens étroits qui se tissèrent à cette époque entre le compositeur et le chef d'orchestre et l'importance du rôle qu'Ansermet devait jouer, par la suite, dans la diffusion mondiale des premières oeuvres de Strawinsky. Ce sera dans cette banale petite villa La Pervenche que commencera à s'élaborer une des partitions majeures de mon père, *Les Noces*. A maintes reprises ajourné, ce travail allait être de nombreuses fois remis sur le chantier au cours des année à venir, tandis que le compositeur menait jusqu'à l'achèvement bien d'autres oeuvres : *Renard*, *L'Histoire du Soldat*, *Ragtime*, *Pulcinella*, *Concertino*, *Symphonies pour Instruments à Vent*, *Mavra* et quelques ouvrages de moindre envergure. La formule instrumentale définitive des *Noces* sera fixée seulement neuf ans plus tard.

Ainsi donc nous sommes en automne 1914 à Clarens. C'est alors et là que se situe l'attristante séparation d'avec ma grand'mère qui décida de regagner notre patrie en guerre. Veuve depuis plus de dix ans, elle vivait tantôt dans son appartement de Saint-Petersbourg qu'elle partageait avec son fils cadet Gouri, tantôt auprès de notre famille qu'elle accompagnait pour quelques semaines ou quelques mois, que ce fut à Oustiloug, en Suisse ou en France . . . Or, l'intrépide oncle Gouri venait de s'engager comme volontaire sur le front des Balkans et elle voulait se rapprocher de lui. Elle avait perdu son aîné Roman. Youri et Igor étaient mariés et pères de famille. C'était sur son cadet qu'elle avait reporté toute la tendresse de son coeur maternel. Vaillamment donc, seule, elle entreprit en pleine guerre le long et périlleux voyage qui devait la conduire de Suisse en Russie en passant par les eaux dangereuses des Dardanelles. Plus tard, fixée à Saint-Petersbourg devenu Leningrad, elle y traversera toute la Révolution et les dures années qui suivirent. Les amis dévoués de ses fils trouveront, pour la protéger et afin qu'elle puisse rester dans son appartement, un heureux et astucieux subterfuge : ils réussiront à la faire nommer concierge de la propre bibliothèque de feu son mari, bibliothèque que le nouveau régime venait d'étatiser.

Après que notre grand'mère nous eût quittés, un court intermède hivernal de deux mois verra notre famille à Château-d'Oex dans les Alpes vaudoises, à l'Hôtel Victoria (1914–15).

N'est-ce pas un miracle que nos parents aient su, au milieu d'une vie aussi mouvementée, créer et préserver pour leurs enfants une vraie et paisible ambiance familiale? Igor, père attentif, bien qu'irritable à l'excès pour des vétilles, un instant si proche, à la chaleur humaine si rassurante, insaisissable l'instant d'après parce que plongé dans le monde secret de la création . . . A ses côtés

Catherine, l'épouse, la mère, douce, d'une grandeur d'âme exceptionnelle, d'une abnégation totale, toujours présente...

Mais la vie nomade que notre famille avait menée en ces sept premières années de mon enfance devait bientôt prendre fin. Le développement de la guerre à l'échelle mondiale obligera maintenant nos parents à envisager en Suisse une installation stable. Le problème scolaire pour la marmaille grandissante les poussera aussi à une décision de ce genre. Et déjà des amitiés solides lient mon père à cette terre romande qui restera son port d'attache jusqu'en 1920. Dans les environs de Lausanne, au bord du Lac Léman, Igor et Catherine choisissent la charmante petite ville de Morges et dès le printemps 1915 ils y louent, avenue des Pâquis, la Villa Rogivue.

A partir de ce moment-là, non seulement le cabinet paternel mais la maison tout entière commencera à se remplir de bibelots et de meubles trouvés au cours de 'descentes' chez les antiquaires et les bric-à-brac de la contrée; heureux temps où l'on pouvait encore y faire de surprenantes trouvailles! Objets qui, par la suite, ayant accompagné la famille dans ses successives installations, deviendront pour nous meubles-souvenirs, objets-souvenirs et dont quelques-uns, à mon grand plaisir, sont depuis plus de trente ans chez moi. Cette table suisse du XVIIIe à l'épais plateau en poirier patiné (achetée déjà à Clarens) et sur laquelle virent le jour tant de partitions du *Sacre* au *Dumbarton Oaks Concerto* ... cette grande armoire peinte au naïf décor polychrômé où mon père rangeait ses manuscrits ... ces gouaches napolitaines rapportées un jour d'Italie ...

A Morges, sur les murs de la Villa Rogivue, les estampes japonaises disparaissent. Elles sont remplacées par les vigoureuses maquettes de Larionov pour *Renard* et par les jolies aquarelles aux couleurs éclatantes que ma mère peignait alors, illustrant le texte des *Noces*. Très douée pour le dessin n'avait-elle pas, comme jeune fille, travaillé avec ses cousines quelques mois à Paris à l'Académie Colarossi?

Ce qui, jusque là, n'avait été pour nous que des noms plus ou moins mystérieux prononcés par les grandes personnes ou, tout au plus, des silhouettes entrevues dans les couloirs d'hôtels, commence à devenir réalité. Des choix s'opèrent dans nos affections d'enfants. Ainsi Diaghilev devient vite 'l'oncle Serge' aux grosses joues rassurantes. Nous nous précipitions à sa rencontre, grimpions sur ses genoux, sachant ses poches toujours pleines de bonbons pour nous. Beaucoup plus tard mon père me raconta qu'il en avait une secrète

réservée aux nombreuses amulettes dont le plus supersticieux des hommes qu'il était ne se séparait jamais. Nijinsky, frêle lui, et le regard perdu, nous laissait indifférents bien que maman nous eût expliqué que ce monsieur était le plus grand danseur du monde et que quand il sautait on eût dit qu'il volait ... De longues heures père s'enfermait avec eux dans son cabinet de travail et au travers de la porte nous parvenaient de tonitruants accords entrecoupés d'éclats de voix parfois si violents qu'ils nous faisaient peur. 'Est-ce qu'ils osent gronder papa?' questionnait, anxieuse, ma sœur Mika (Ludmila) et grand était notre soulagement étonné lorsque ces trois grandes personnes ressortaient sourire aux lèvres.

Diaghilev, Nijinsky, Massine, Larionov, Gontcharova, Prokofiev et quelques autres c'était le monde des Ballets-Russes; amitiés qui avaient pris racine en Russie. A ceux-ci joignons encore Basile Kibaltchitch, chef de chœur. Tous, comme mes parents, subissaient maintenant, par la force des choses, le sort commun des émigrés. A Morges vont se sceller des amitiés nouvelles qui joueront dès lors dans la vie de mon père un rôle tout aussi important. Ernest Ansermet, l'écrivain C.-F. Ramuz, le peintre René Auberjonois, Henri Bischoff un autre peintre, Jean Morax peintre lui aussi et son frère le dramaturge René Morax, Alexandre Cingria un peintre encore et Charles-Albert Cingria son frère, ce grand poète trop peu connu ... Ceux-ci formaient le noyau de tout un cercle d'amis que mes parents avaient toujours plaisir à accueillir dans leur maison toujours ouverte et à leur table toujours servie. Si les soucis de l'heure ne faisaient pas défaut, la chaude hospitalité russe ne perdait pas ses droits. Innombrables ont été les amis qui défilèrent sous le toit morgien des Strawinsky.

Ma mémoire conserve et confond avec bonheur et attendrissement nos Noëls scintillants et nos Pâques à la russe, sans oublier ce Nouvel-An où père et mère se déguisèrent pour notre amusement. Le chef de famille apparut en rapin, béret à la Rembrandt, cravate Lavallière, chevalet sur l'épaule, palette et pinceaux à la main ...

Pour nous les enfants la vie s'écoule selon le rythme scolaire. A la maison, le matin, on marche sur la pointe des pieds ... Strawinsky compose. Mais voilà que la femme de chambre, oubliant la consigne du silence, se met à chanter, si ce n'est la cuisinière à siffler! Il n'en faut pas davantage pour provoquer les foudres du compositeur et ma mère d'user de toute sa diplomatie pour calmer son époux ... et garder ses domestiques! L'après-midi, en revanche, l'atmosphère est à la détente. Le plus souvent mon père orchestre; à ses côtés, heures paisibles, ma mère recopie partitions ou réductions pour piano jusqu'à notre retour de l'école. C'est alors la leçon de russe. Tandis que j'écris sous sa dictée ou lui lis quelque passage, je vois encore le petit outil à l'aide duquel agilement elle confectionne, avec un tabac spécial qui embaumait toute la maison, les cigarettes de prédilection de mon père. Il les fumait au bout d'un long fume-cigarettes légèrement courbé 'en bec d'albatros', nous disait-on, 'très, très précieux!' Avec nos parents, nous les enfants avons toujours parlé le russe. A l'école et entre nous c'était le français; l'allemand avec les gouvernantes.

Si la vie était maintenant devenue sédentaire pour les siens, notre père lui, ne cessait de voyager. Les occasions, liées à l'activité des Ballets-Russes, ne manquaient pas bien que les déplacements fussent géographiquement limités par l'extension des hostilités. L'amitié de Strawinsky pour Diaghilev était réelle et grande l'admiration réciproque des deux hommes. Toutefois mon père ne se faisait guère d'illusions sur les tentations que présentait pour lui cette ambiance. Déjà dans une lettre datée d'Oustiloug 14–X–1912 et adressée à son ami Maurice Delage on peut lire, entre autres, à propos de ses rapports avec les Ballets-Russes, cette étonnante confession: ' . . . *la gloire et l'argent dont les tentations rongent insensiblement mes entrailles . . .*' On y voit encore qu'il ne se faisait pas davantage d'illusions quant au climat frelaté et aux intrigues qui régnaient dans les coulisses de l'illustre compagnie et quant à l'atmosphère de snobisme qui la soutenait. Mais la vie est ce qu'elle est: sa nature profonde et son art ont toujours posé à Strawinsky une double et contradictoire exigence. Débordant de la plus extra-ordinaire vitalité, cet homme tourné vers l'extérieur moins en vue de la diffusion de ses oeuvres que par un réel besoin de contact direct avec le public-auditeur, n'était-ce pas le même qui trouvait dans le cadre de la vie familiale le climat idéal pour leur élaboration? Il en résultait une vie de famille réelle, intime, mais avec la constante alternance de ses voyages pour rejoindre ici ou là Diaghilev et sa troupe, puis, plus tard, de ses tournées de concerts. Cette vie sur deux plans durera jusqu'à l'hiver 1938–39 au cours duquel, en l'espace de six mois tragiques, il perdra successivement sa fille Ludmila, sa femme et sa mère. Plus de foyer, la famille se disloque . . . chacun de nous fera sa propre vie et notre père refera la sienne en épousant aux Etats-Unis en 1940 Véra Soudeikine, née de Bosset.

Mais revenons à Morges aux années 1915–1916. Auprès de notre mère nous attendions, avec la plus grande impatience, le retour – que ce fut de Rome, de Madrid ou de Paris – de notre père voyageur. Il nous rapportait toujours quelque cadeau imprévu: tel ce disque d'une corrida où les fanfares, les *ole*! de la foule et surtout le beuglement du taureau nous tenaient en haleine tandis que Père, tout de muscles sur une frêle charpente, nous mimait des passes de torrero avec le plaid rouge toujours jeté sur son canapé. En souvenir de son premier contact avec l'Espagne Strawinsky composera bientôt une pièce pour pianola intitulée *Madrid*. Dans une version instrumentale il l'inserrera plus tard dans ses *Quatre Etudes pour Orchestre*. Et plus tard encore l'excellent pianiste que sera devenu son propre fils Soulima fera de ce *Madrid* de notre enfance une transcription pour deux pianos.

Et puis il y a l' Española' des *Cinq Pièces Faciles* qui évoquent irréstiblement pour moi (tout comme les *Trois Pièces Faciles*) nos premiers contacts avec le piano, les premiers pas, dirais-je, de nos doigts d'enfants sur le clavier, les premières lectures des notes sur la portée. Et c'est aussi le beau 'bleu de lessive' des murs du cabinet de travail paternel où chacun de nous, à tour de rôle, venait s'asseoir vingt minutes devant le piano droit, sur le tabouret à vis, toujours arrêté assez haut pour nous empêcher de toucher aux pédales; cruelle tentation! Notre professeur? Père lui-même, Igor Strawinsky faisant preuve là, avec ses petits élèves, d'une patience étonnante, ou mieux: dominant je pense – j'en suis même certain – une impatience naturelle. Cette impatience dominée, ne la retrouverons nous pas, chez cet homme qui fut un impatient par excellence, dans ses rapports avec les musiciens d'orchestre?

Un jour notre père revient d'une course à Genève tout à la joie d'y avoir déniché un cymbalum hongrois, instrument rare auquel il rêvait depuis quelque temps déjà, voulant l'introduire dans la partition de *Renard* à laquelle il travaillait. Toujours ce besoin de contact direct avec la matière sonore. Je vois encore l'arrivée à la maison de cet objet inconnu. A peine déballé dans la cour – c'est là que notre père nous le fit entendre – ce jouet pour grandes personnes nous enchanta et chacun à son tour fut admis à l'étrenner. Mais dès qu'il eût rejoint dans le cabinet paternel la place qui lui était impartie, il ne fallut plus y toucher! A l'époque de *l'Histoire du Soldat* c'est de toute une batterie qu'il fera ainsi l'acquisition. La grosse caisse, à en juger par la couleur – alternance de triangles verts et blancs — ne pouvait que sortir de quelque fanfare de village vaudois.

A la fin de l'année 1915, très exactement le 20 décembre, Serge de Diaghilev organise, au profit de la Croix-Rouge Internationale à Genève, berceau de cette Institution, un grand spectacle de gala. Date mémorable pour Igor Strawinsky, ce soir-là il dirigera pour la première fois en public. Au programme, sous sa baguette une suite symphonique de fragments de *l'Oiseau de Feu;* sous celle d'Ansermet les ballets *Carnaval*, d'après Schumann et *Soleil de Nuit* de Rimsky-Korsakov. Quelles ne furent pas ma surprise, ma joie et ma fierté lorsque mes parents m'annoncèrent qu'ils me prendraient avec eux au spectacle! En costume du dimanche, en souliers vernis j'arrivai au Grand-Théâtre. Les yeux écarquillés du petit garçon visuel et imaginatif que je devais être buvaient avidement tout pêle-mêle: le rideau, la scène, la salle, son lustre, les rouges, les ors; la salle dans l'obscurité, la scène sous les feux de la rampe et à mes côtés, dans la loge d'avant-scène, si jolie dans sa robe bleu pâle, ma mère. Et puis la fosse d'orchestre, ce grand trou noir aux petites lumières, d'où, sous les applaudissements, surgit soudain, souple et légère, la silhouette de mon père. D'un bond le voilà au pupitre. Il salue bas, se retourne et, posément, délibérément, casse la baguette. J'en eus le souffle coupé . . . il la trouvait simplement trop longue! Puis Monsieur Ansermet à la barbe si noire sur le plastron blanc. A l'entr'acte, les parquets luisants et glissants, les messieurs en frac, les dames parfumées et les gendarmes genevois en grande tenue, chapeau bicorne, épaulettes, aiguillettes, baudrier et gants blancs . . . Les lustres scintillants se reflétant à l'infini dans les immenses glaces du foyer . . . Et comment oublierais-je l'apparition dans notre loge de la grande dame toute blanche qui, tout à l'heure, à l'ouverture du spectacle avait chanté devant le rideau l'hymne national russe 'Dieu garde-nous le Tzar'? Felia Litvine, qui fut jadis une des gloires de l'Opéra Impérial de Saint-Petersbourg, se pencha vers moi, me serra contre son ample poitrine et me chuchota à l'oreille en russe: 'Tu sais, petit Théodore, quand tu n'étais pas né encore j'ai chanté avec le grand Théodore ton grand-père'. Je sens la curieuse odeur vanillée du cosmetique qu'elle avait sur son visage. J'étais un peu intimidé . . . Puis enfin devant le rideau, l'oncle Serge saluant, tenant les jolies danseuses par la main . . . Que d'émotions, que d'impressions nouvelles! Miracle de la faculté d'absorption d'un petit être humain, confronté pour la première fois avec tout un monde de rêve et de merveilleux devenu subitement réalité et aussitôt gravé à jamais dans sa mémoire.

A Morges, sous le toit paternel, la famille s'était enrichie de la présence de notre chère vieille Bertha Essert, d'origine allemande, que mon père avait pu 'récupérer' malgré les hostilités. Entrée dans la famille Strawinsky dès avant la naissance d'Igor elle avait été la fidèle niania de son enfance. Il n'y avait de gâteries qu'elle n'ait eues jadis pour lui et pour ses frères, qu'elle n'avait maintenant pour nous les enfants d'Igor. Mais qu'est-ce donc au juste qu'une niania? Ce n'est pas un diplôme, ce n'est pas une fonction, pas même celle d'intendante que parfois elle assume. C'est, dirais-je, un état qu'elle acquiert. Il n'était pas de famille russe tant soit peu aisée qui n'eût sa niania, être indispensable au confort moral d'une famille, sorte de doublure des grand'mamans mais dont nul ne songeait à prendre ombrage car elle ne supplantait personne. Bien au contraire, une niania complétait la traditionnelle famille russe, elle lui donnait une certaine rondeur. Une niania acquiert droit de famille comme on acquiert droit de cité par un long dévouement à la cause commune. Elle terminera ses jours entourée du respect et de l'amour d'une, deux ou même trois générations. Certaines nianias sont restées célèbres, nous pensons à celle de Pouchkine que le poète chanta en d'inoubliables vers. La bonne chère Bertha fut la nôtre, comme elle avait été celle de notre père; nous l'aimions comme une vraie grand'maman. Elle s'éteignit subitement par un bel après-midi du printemps 1917. Une grande agitation régna dans la maison, puis tout-à-coup ce fut un grand silence. On parla bas, on marcha sur la pointe des pieds. Des hommes inconnus circulaient dans l'escalier. Je voyais pour la première fois père et mère pleurer à chaudes-larmes, les amis intimes envelopper mes parents d'une étrange prévenance . . . Un pasteur luthérien en longue redingote noire arriva et la déférence triste que lui témoignait mon père me frappa . . . C'était la première fois que j'étais placé devant la réalité mystérieuse de la mort. Et pourtant, peu auparavant, n'avais-je pas en quelque sorte déjà pris conscience de son existence? La niania de ma mère et de sa soeur, Sophie Velsovsky – Baba Sonia – ne s'était-elle pas, elle aussi, éteinte mais au loin, en Russie, chez les Beliankine. Je rentrais de l'école; je trouvai maman en larmes et papa qui la consolait avec une grande tendresse. 'Baba Sonia est morte, nous ne la reverrons plus . . .' Cette chère Baba Sonia inséparable de tous nos souvenirs d'avant 1914 . . .

La Villa Rogivue était devenue bien triste. C'est alors que Mina Svitalski entra chez nous comme gouvernante pour les aînés. A son tour elle ne tardera pas à devenir notre nouvelle niania; ce sera la si sensible, l'inoubliable Madubo, surnom que lui donna mon frère en la voyant et qui devint aussitôt son nom pour nous tous et pour tous nos amis. Elle devait rester sa vie durant auprès des uns et des autres d'entre nous. Et lorsqu'elle nous eût élevés tous quatre, ne berça-t-elle pas encore la petite Catherine, fille de Ludmila et le petit John, fils de Soulima? Et après qu'elle eût passé plus de quarante ans parmi les Strawinsky il m'échut de recueillir son dernier soupir.

L'été 1917, Bertha disparue, mes parents éprouvèrent le besoin de changer de cadre. Toujours très à la russe, la maisonnée se transporta à la montagne, aux Diablerets dans les Alpes vaudoises. Précédant le cortège, le piano; ensuite valises et paquets; le chien Mouche et toute une basse-cour dans des cages d'osier; cuisinière, femme de chambre, gouvernante, Madubo, papa, maman et leurs quatre enfants. Le chalet Les Fougères nous accueillit tous. Le propriétaire, un brave menuisier en retraite, laissait 'le monsieur russe, un original' s'installer dans ce qui avait été son atelier. Aux murs étonnés de cet insolite cabinet de travail, ne voit-on pas aussitôt apparaître les photographies des extraordinaires 'hommes-sandwiches' créés par Picasso pour *Parade*, le ballet d'Erik Satie et Jean Cocteau que Diaghilev venait de monter à Rome. Là, sur l'établi même de l'artisan, Strawinsky travailla tout l'été au dernier tableau des *Noces*.

Par la verrière de cet atelier j'entrevis une fois un visage encore inconnu: un monsieur à la face pâle, plate, ronde et glâbre, portant de grosses lunettes, parlait véhémentement avec mon père. Puis ils jouèrent aux cartes au fond du jardin sous une tonnelle. Et quand le monsieur, drapé dans une ample cape de loden, fut raccompagné à la petite gare du village, notre père au retour nous dit: 'Il était furieux parce qu'il a tout le temps perdu!' Et pourtant, à nous, on nous disait qu'il ne fallait jamais se fâcher quand on perdait au jeu! Le perdant de l'après-midi était André Gide. Si, bien des années plus tard, en 1933, il y aura pour *Perséphone* une collaboration Strawinsky-Gide, bien qu'elle sera l'occasion de nombreuses rencontres, elle ne pourra rapprocher deux natures que séparait un abîme.

Une autre visite: celle de Jacques Copeau, accompagné de sa fille Mayenne, de peu notre aînée et dont les beaux longs cheveux blonds me faisaient rêver...

Le temps, particulièrement beau cet été-là, incitait souvent mon père à se joindre à nos petites excursions. Un jour, après un long après-midi de cueillette de framboises dans les bois, chacun portant son seau plein du léger et parfumé petit fruit, nous rentrions joyeusement aux Fougères. J'entends encore mes parents dire: 'Vraiment quelle merveilleuse journée!' A ce moment précis un télégraphiste à bicyclette nous rejoignit. Père lut la dépêche, la passa à ma mère. 'Oncle Gouri est mort', dit maman. 'Très loin, là-bas, sur le front roumain', ajouta lentement mon père. Il prit la main de ma mère, en silence nous rentrâmes. Le lien de sang qui existait entre les époux Igor et Catherine Strawinsky, puisqu'ils étaient cousins germains, leur faisait ressentir à l'unisson les deuils comme les joies de famille.

De retour à Morges, nos parents durent faire face à un souci inattendu: la Villa Rogivue que nous habitions depuis mai 1915 venait d'être brusquement vendue par son propriétaire. Il fallait donc de nouveau déménager et rapidement. Par bonheur ils trouvèrent à deux pas un spacieux et charmant appartement dans la belle demeure XVIIIe dite 'Maison Bornand', place St. Louis. Nous les enfants, devions dire adieu au grand jardin, depuis plus de deux ans témoin de nos jeux.

Pour Igor et Catherine une vie désormais sans contact avec la patrie se prolonge douloureusement. Après la Révolution d'octobre il leur faudra se convaincre que la séparation est, hélas! définitive. Voilà sans doute qui explique suffisamment, par une légitime nostalgie, le véritable engouement de Strawinsky à cette époque pour la poésie populaire russe dont il explore et exploite amoureusement les inépuisables richesses. De ce folklore il fera véritablement sa chose. *Pribaoutki*, *Berceuses du Chat*, *Quatre Chants Russes*, *Les Noces*, *Renard*, toutes ces oeuvres vocales ne témoignent-elles pas d'une sorte d'accaparement créateur?

Ici se place la collaboration de mon père avec C.F.Ramuz. Il s'agissait pour Strawinsky d'avoir moins une traduction de ses textes qu'une version française ne trahissant pas la prosodie qu'il avait établie en russe. Seules une sensibilité et une intuition de poète comme celles de Ramuz – parce qu'elles vibraient, tant sur le plan humain qu'esthétique, au même diapason, peut-on dire, que celles de Strawinsky – permirent aux deux amis, par une sorte de prodige, de mener à bonne fin un projet qui eût dû leur paraître insensé: l'auteur de la version française ignorant tout de la langue russe! Or cette collaboration s'avéra la plus réciproquement satisfaisante qui se puisse concevoir. Il n'est, pour s'en convaincre, que de se référer à ce qu'en dit Strawinsky lui-même dans ses *Chroniques* ainsi qu'aux admirables pages qu'y consacre Ramuz dans ses *Souvenirs sur Igor Strawinsky*.

Strawinsky comme Ramuz s'est toujours méfié des théories. Attachés qu'ils étaient tous deux au concret, leurs conversations sur les choses de l'art ne prenaient jamais tournure de dissertation. Les rencontres des deux amis étaient devenues presque quotidiennes. Tôt le matin, quand nous n'étions pas à l'école, nous aimions aller chercher à la gare Monsieur Ramuz et c'est le dernier train du soir qui le ramenait chez lui à Lausanne.

Venons-en maintenant au fruit essentiel de la conjonction Strawinsky-Ramuz: *L'Histoire du Soldat*. Le texte, cette fois-ci, sera intégralement créé par Ramuz, le thème emprunté à un conte populaire russe que Strawinsky raconte à son ami, l'histoire transplantée en un pays de Vaud imaginaire. Une petite paranthèse: mon père aimait à raconter qu'une certaine nuit de 1918, à l'époque où il travaillait à *L'Histoire du Soldat*, il vit en rêve une belle Bohémienne assise à la porte de sa roulotte. Tout en donnant le sein à son enfant, la jeune femme jouait sur un violon un air de tango. 'C'est la seule fois – disait Igor Strawinsky – que je parvins à capter et à noter intégralement à mon réveil une phrase musicale nettement entendue en rêve, car les rêves musicaux se volatilisent au réveil.' Le thème de la Bohémienne devint le Tango de *L'Histoire du Soldat*. Comme le dira l'affiche, la pièce sera 'lue, jouée et dansée'. Les difficultés matérielles de l'heure imposaient l'économie. Trois acteurs-danseurs, un lecteur et sept musiciens. Conditions qui amenèrent le compositeur à créer, dans un dépouillement concerté, un langage musical nouveau.

Quatre amis se réunissaient sous notre toît: Strawinsky, Ramuz, Ansermet et René Auberjonois; celui-ci fera décors et costumes. A la table familiale l'humeur paternelle était le fidèle baromètre de ces rencontres souvent houleuses: beau, variable, tempête . . . mais l'enthousiasme présida à tout le travail préparatoire. La représentation eût lieu le 29 septembre 1918 à Lausanne. Ce spectacle procura à mon père, il l'écrira lui-même plus tard, la plus grande satisfaction qu'il eût jamais éprouvée à la réalisation d'une de ses oeuvres scéniques.

Combien j'étais, moi, heureux et fier vis-à-vis des petits camarades de collège endimanchés qui occupaient, avec leurs parents, la loge voisine. Et comment ne mentionnerais-je pas ici,

puisqu'il s'agit de souvenirs, l'inoubliable lecteur que fut Elie Gagnebin? sa lecture, véritable jeu, nous enthousiasma. L'amitié fidèle qui le liera à toute notre famille datera de *L'Histoire du Soldat*. Pour les tournées envisagées on était donc à l'optimisme en cette fin de septembre 1918 et pourtant cette Première devait rester, pour bien des années, l'unique représentation de l'oeuvre. La terrible épidémie qui sévissait alors à travers toute l'Europe sous le nom de 'grippe espagnole' s'abattit soudain sur auteurs, acteurs et musiciens. Tout le monde dût se mettre au lit. A la maison, je vois mon père enfoui sous ses couvertures, claquant des dents, béret basque enfoncé jusqu'aux yeux, ne décolérant pas. Je vois ma mère chancelante, en robe de chambre, administrant à tous, petits et grands, potions, tisanes, sirops . . . La tournée envisagée était définitivement compromise; l'oeuvre, elle, devait faire glorieusement son chemin plus tard, ailleurs et autrement.

Bien que *L'Histoire du Soldat* soit sans conteste une des oeuvres capitales de la production strawinskienne et que Serge de Diaghilev fût certainement un des premiers admirateurs de mon père, ce pionnier, ce novateur, cet homme au flair de fin limier bouda l'oeuvre nouvelle. Elle n'avait pas été placée sous son égide. Le poulain favori n'allait-il pas s'échapper de son écurie?

Nous arrivons maintenant à la dernière année de notre vie à Morges. La guerre est terminée. Les voyages de mon père à Paris se font de plus en plus fréquents. Dans mes souvenirs cette période reste dominée par l'oeuvre principale à laquelle travaillait alors Strawinsky: *Pulcinella*. De l'un de ses voyages il avait rapporté une collection d'ouvrages inachevés et de fragments inédits de Pergolèse, matériel glâné par Diaghilev dans diverses bibliothèques d'Europe et qui devait fournir au compositeur la substance musicale de base pour un nouveau ballet. C'est alors que s'installe, dans le quotidien de la famille Strawinsky, le nom déjà prestigieux de Pablo Picasso. Si, depuis quelques années, ce dernier était un ami de mon père, à l'occasion du ballet de *Pulcinella*, pour lequel il fera décor et costumes, s'établiront entre le musicien et le peintre des rapports plus étroits. L'affrontement dans la collaboration d'un trio tel que Diaghilev-Strawinsky-Picasso ne pouvait que provoquer des étincelles susceptibles d'embraser un ciel tout entier. Mais la confiance réciproque née de l'admiration que ces trois grands avaient l'un pour l'autre surmonta les obstacles et aboutit à une des plus hautes réussites des Ballets-Russes. La figure de Picasso nous devient alors familière; elle se concrétise à la maison par une série de dessins, de gouaches et de peintures données par le peintre à mes parents. Au célèbre portrait du compositeur de face, au crayon et dédicacé: 'A Strawinsky de son ami Picasso' ma mère donnera sur nos murs la place d'honneur.

Si loin que je me reporte dans mes souvenirs d'enfance je ne me vois pas ayant jamais varié dans mon désir d'être peintre 'quand je serai grand'. Le contact avec l'oeuvre de Picasso et bientôt avec l'homme aura pour moi l'effet d'un véritable réactif. Auprès de mes parents, tous deux si sensibles aux arts plastiques, comme auprès de leurs amis peintres je ne trouvais qu'encouragement, ma voie était tracée. Celle de mon frère ne devait pas tarder à l'être à son tour. Dès sa tendre enfance Soulima voulut être pianiste et à cette indubitable vocation mon père applaudit. Très tôt le propre fils d'Igor Strawinsky interprétera dans le monde entier, entre autres, le répertoire pianistique paternel. Mais n'anticipons pas ... si ce n'est pour noter au passage que l'arrière-petit-fils de Feodor Ignatievitch Strawinsky, John, petit-fils d'Igor, fils de Soulima, fait preuve, lui, d'une réelle vocation d'acteur...

Revenons à Morges, nous sommes en 1920. Les circonstances internationales de l'après-guerre ouvraient à la carrière brillante de l'artiste encore jeune qu'était alors mon père un champ d'activité nouveau. Il ne pouvait plus s'accommoder de notre résidence dans la délicieuse petite ville vaudoise où les hostilités mondiales avaient confiné notre vie de famille. Après avoir un temps songé à Rome, mes parents décidèrent de transporter leurs pénates à Paris. Mais aux Strawinsky, à eux seuls déjà nombreux, il fallait maintenant ajouter la famille de mon oncle Beliankine qui, après mille détours et aventures, avait pu sortir de Russie et venir nous rejoindre à Morges. Les deux soeurs si unies qu'étaient ma mère et ma tante se retrouvaient enfin et nous, nous récupérions cousin et cousine. Ainsi, une fois de plus, ce sera à la tête d'une vraie tribu que mon père, en vrai patriarche – mais la barbe c'est notre oncle qui la portait! – embarquera tout son monde de Morges à Paris vers une destination nouvelle...

Les préparatifs de départ ne furent pas, comme bien l'on pense, une petite affaire. Mon père pensait à tout, s'affairait; ma mère, assistée de Madubo, vaquait aux détails pratiques; nous, les enfants, faisions nos visites d'adieu, prenions congé de nos camarades, de nos maîtres d'école...

L'appartement de la Maison Bornand est sens-dessus-dessous. Valises, coffres, caisses, paille, courants d'air, déménageurs et verres de vin. Faute de sièges, c'est assis sur des caisses que l'on bavarde avec les amis qui se succèdent, accourent pour dire au revoir. J'entends: 'Alors Ramuz, vous ne partez pas avec nous?' – 'Voyons, Strawinsky, vous n'y pensez pas! C'est horriblement loin Paris ... et je ne suis pas un globe-trotter comme vous!' Ton que Ramuz affectait volontiers...

Avec le recul des ans il apparaît clairement, comme je l'écrivais en tête de cet album, que l'on peut sans trop d'arbitraire diviser la vie de mon père en trois parties dont la première s'achève sans nul doute précisément en ce début d'été 1920 où la Suisse, Morges, vont être quittés.

Arrive le grand jour du départ. Nous sommes plus d'une douzaine, grands et petits, à nous répartir dans je ne sais combien de compartiments. Arrêt à Genève où l'on va prendre dans quelques heures le train de nuit pour Paris. Les Ansermet, les bras chargés de petits cadeaux, viennent à la gare. D'autres amis encore sur le quai agiteront leur mouchoir. En attendant le départ, on mange des sandwiches au buffet. Aux petits on donne de la grenadine, mais à moi, mon père, me considérant ce jour-là comme un grand, sérieusement, me verse mon premier *vrai boc de bière*. Ce geste paternel, je le vois encore aujourd'hui. Retenons-le peut-être comme l'un des derniers souvenirs de mon enfance. Irrésistiblement il me reporte au tout premier souvenir de ma toute première enfance.

Et une fois de plus dans les annales de notre famille, sur un quai de gare, on compte et recompte paquets et valises mais surtout, ô! surtout on ne perd pas de vue celle qui, lourde à plus d'un titre et précieuse entre toutes, contient les manuscrits déjà si nombreux d'Igor Strawinsky.

Théodore Strawinsky

Vorwort

Man kann, wie mir scheint, ohne allzu grosse Willkür das Leben
meines Vaters Igor Strawinsky in drei verschiedene Abschnitte
einteilen.

Der erste, der bis 1920 geht und das Thema dieses Albums
darstellt, könnte 'Von Russland in den Westen' heissen.

Der zweite entspräche dem Leben des Komponisten und seiner
Familie in Frankreich von 1920 bis 1939.

Der dritte endlich, von 1939 bis zu seinem Tode 1971, würde sich
über die Jahre erstrecken, die mein Vater in den Vereinigten
Staaten verbrachte.

Es ist also ausschliesslich der erste Abschnitt dieses langen Lebens,
den die folgenden kurzen Beschreibungen eher zu evozieren als
zu erzählen suchen. Sie bewegen sich um Kindheitserinnerungen,
um Gesehenes, Erlebtes und so in meinem Gedächtnis Bewahrtes,
gestützt durch das, was ich unmittelbar von meinen Eltern über die
Meinen weiss, und sie begleiten eine Auswahl von zumeist
unveröffentlichten Familienphotos, die ich von meiner Mutter
habe. Das Ganze – Text und Photos – bildet so gleichsam eine
Reihe von Blitzlichtern, die das Familienleben meines Vaters
bis 1920 erhellen und sich somit über die Zeit meiner Kindheit
erstrecken. Es ist also nicht verwunderlich, dass die Musik hier nur
am Rande erscheinen wird. Die Werke meines Vaters werden nur
als chronologische Anhaltspunkte zitiert werden.

Fünf Photographien schliesslich, die meine Frau in Evian Ende
August 1970, also wenige Monate nur vor dem Tode meines Vaters
aufgenommen hat, werden als ergreifender Epilog dieses
'Familienalbum' abschliessen.

Igor und Katharina Strawinsky, meine Eltern, im Mittelpunkt meiner Kindheitserinnerungen

F eodor Ignatjewitsch und Anna Kyrillowna, die Eltern Igor Strawinskys, gehörten am Ende des letzten Jahrhunderts fest zu den Musikerkreisen von Petersburg, der damaligen Hauptstadt Russlands.

Feodor Ignatjewitsch Strawinsky (Theodor, Sohn des Ignaz), 1843 geboren, entstammte einer alten Familie polnischen Ursprungs. Er machte als Bass am Marientheater, der kaiserlichen Oper, Karriere. Der sehr grosse Umfang seiner warmen und ergreifenden Stimme und seine aussergewöhnliche schauspielerische Begabung brachten ihm sehr früh grossen Ruhm. Als aufgeschlossener Geist war er bestrebt, den Staub der veralteten Routine von der ehrwürdigen Petersburger Bühne wegzufegen, und führte als Neuerer einen realistischen und lebendigen Stil ein. Theodor Strawinsky, mein Grossvater, verlieh der russischen Opernbühne seiner Zeit ein stark persönliches Gepräge. Als kultivierter Literaturkenner baute er sich eine bedeutende Bibliothek auf.

Seine Gattin, Anna Kyrillowna (Anna, Tochter des Kyrill) geborene Cholodowsky, besass ihrerseits einen hübschen Mezzosopran, nützte ihn jedoch nicht beruflich, sondern begnügte sich damit, zu ihrem eigenen Vergnügen zu singen; sie war sehr musikalisch. Sollte nicht ihr Sohn Igor eines Tages sagen: 'Von ihr habe ich die kostbare Gabe, Orchesterpartituren zu lesen.'

Vorbildlich als Paar, als Eltern jedoch vielleicht allzu anspruchsvoll, hatten Theodor und Anna Strawinsky einige Schwierigkeiten bei der Erziehung ihrer vier unbändigen Söhne: Roman, Juri, Igor und Guri.

Herzliche Familienbeziehungen verbanden diese mit ihren zahlreichen Vettern Jellatschitsch und ihren ebenso zahlreichen Kusinen Nossenko. Jeden Sommer traf man sich mit Freude auf den Landgütern der einen oder der anderen.

In Petersburg, der schönen Hauptstadt der Zaren, mit ihrer Architektur im Palladio-Stil verbrachten Igor und seine Brüder ihre Kindheit und Jugend. Hier studierte Igor Jura, um sich den vernünftigen Forderungen seiner Eltern zu beugen; Musik, um dem herrischen Drang seiner einzigen Neigung nachzugeben. In Petersburg auch verbanden sich am 24. Januar 1906 Igor Feodorowitsch Strawinsky und Jekaterina Gawrilowna Nossenko (Katharina, Tochter des Gabriel), seine Kusine, fürs Leben, hier verbrachten sie die ersten drei Jahre ihrer Ehe, und hier erblickten ihre ersten beiden Kinder, Theodor und Ludmilla, 1907–1908 das Licht der Welt.

1910. Winter, ein junger siebenundzwanzigjähriger Mann, über den kleinen, blässlichen, kaum dreijährigen Jungen, der ich war, gebeugt, singt scherzend in fröhlichem Takt: 'Bier her, Bier her!', um ihm auf ärztliche Verordnung einen vollen Löffel Ochsenblut einzugeben. Das Spielchen wiederholte sich bei jeder Mahlzeit und das Schreckliche wurde ... Musik! Schon damals war Igor väterlich und um seinen Erstgeborenen Theodor rührend besorgt. Dies ist die älteste Erinnerung, die mein heute sechzigjähriges Gedächtnis an meinen Vater bewahrt hat.

Davor keinerlei Erinnerung, ausser dieser drolligen kleinen Geschichte, die ich von meinem Vater selbst habe: als ich geboren wurde und meine Mutter mich nicht stillen konnte, musste man in aller Eile eine Amme finden. Man sah sich die Annoncen an, Igor ging in ein Stellenvermittlungsbüro, und dort wurden ihm mehrere junge Personen vorgestellt, die sämtliche mit blosser Brust angetreten waren; daraufhin spritzte jede einzelne der Reihe nach einige Tropfen ihrer kostbaren Flüssigkeit in einen kleinen Becher, der dem jungen Vater zum Kosten gereicht wurde. Ich weiss nicht, wie er seine Auswahl traf, aber die Auserwählte befriedigte, scheint es, vollkommen ...

Das Klima der grossen nordischen Stadt, wo der harte Winter sich endlos in die Länge zieht, während der Sommer mit seinen schwülen, weissen Nächten wie im Traum vergeht, war der zarten Gesundheit meiner Mutter nicht zuträglich. Bald schon sollte sich mein Vater Gedanken deshalb machen. Die Petersburger Wohnung am Engländerprospekt beherbergte nicht mehr lange das junge Paar. Schon 1910 beschliessen meine Eltern, die Ufer der Newa zu verlassen. Von da an kam mein Vater nur noch allein zu kurzem Arbeitsaufenthalt zurück. Die Familie aber, die ständig wuchs – es gab bereits Njanjas, Gouvernanten, Onkeln, Tanten, Grossmütter und sollte sie auch weiterhin geben –, führte nun bis zum Krieg von 1914 ein ständiges Wanderleben. Igor und Katharina hatten in Ustilug in Wolhynien, im äussersten Südwesten Russlands, auf Ländereien, die meiner Mutter und ihrer Schwester Ludmilla gehörten, einen Land- und Sommersitz gebaut, der unsere Familie jeden Sommer bis zum Herbst 1913 beherbergen sollte, und alljährlich zog zur schlechten Jahreszeit der ganze Hausstaat unter mildere Himmel nach Westeuropa: in die Schweiz oder an die französische Riviera. So wurde von 1909 bis 1914 meine frühe Kindheit von ständigem Hin-und-Her beherrscht. Petersburg-Ustilug, Ustilug-La Baule, Clarens, Beaulieu, Ustilug, Clarens . . .

Verweilen wir jedoch ein wenig in Ustilug, an das sich die köstlichsten Erinnerungen meiner ersten Jahre knüpfen. Dinge und Ereignisse beginnen sich jetzt immer deutlicher meinem Gedächtnis einzuprägen. Die Sommer von Ustilug entzückten mich. Sie überfluten in der Rückschau meine Kindheit mit einem glücklichen Licht.

Die neugepflanzten Bäume spendeten einen kühlen, leichten Schatten um das Haus. Ein einfacher Holzzaun trennte uns von unseren Vettern; die Schwester meiner Mutter hatte einen Marineoffizier, Gregor Beljankin, geheiratet, dem sie zwei Kinder schenkte: eine Tochter und einen Sohn, Ira und Ganja. Eine innige Zuneigung verband meine Mutter und meine Tante: es war das lebendige Band zwischen unseren Familien. Die beiden Häuser standen nebeneinander. Wenn das unsere schlicht war, so schien mir das Beljankinsche mit seinem eckigen Turm und seinem halbkreisförmigen, unvollendeten (und auch später nie fertig gebauten!) Säulengang der Inbegriff von Pracht zu sein . . ., und weiter hinten, jener geheimnisvolle Ort, jener vergitterte Zwinger, in dem vier riesige Berhardinerhunde ständig auf etwas zu warten schienen . . . Und nun erst der knatternde, phantastische Dedion-Bouton meines Onkels, mit den riesigen Messingscheinwerfern! Ich empfand es als Erniedrigung, dass meine Eltern nicht auch einen solchen besassen. Mit welcher Wonne drückte ich auf den riesigen Gummiball der Hupe, die die überempfindlichen Ohren der Grossen betäubte! Während ich hoch auf dem Moleskinsitz neben meinem Onkel thronte, ging es in sausendem Wind rund um die Grünflächen, wie mir schien in rasender Fahrt . . . Vor dem väterlichen Haus hingegen und unter dem Fenster meines Vaters hiess es stille sein. Sein Arbeitszimmer, ein grosser viereckiger Raum, in den ich gern hineinschlüpfte, ist mir noch heute, bis auf das kleinste Detail, gegenwärtig. Die mit Bildern bedeckten Wände, das hohe Pult, der Empireschreibtisch mit den grossen Schubladen, die Federn und Bleistifte, Lineale und Radiergummis, verschiedenfarbige Tinte in kleinen Kristallfläschchen, Radiermesser in verschiedener Grösse und Form, japanische Briefbeschwerer . . . Lauter Dinge, die um so verlockender waren, als man sie nie berühren durfte! In diesem Sanktum, wo mir alles wunderbar erschien, lernte ich eines Tages in Form einer Radierung Alexander Puschkin kennen. Vor dem Bildnis des

Dichters erklärte mir mein Vater, wer dieser Herr sei und was das bedeute, ein Schriftsteller. Puschkin heisst auf russisch *von der Kanone*, und das machte mir den grössten Eindruck. Auf dem grossen Flügel, an dem er kürzlich zur Hochzeit von Rimsky-Korsakovs Tochter das *Feuerwerk* komponiert hatte, hatte mein Vater immer eine Partitur in Arbeit. Hatte nicht der alte Meister eines Tages seinem jungen Schüler auf die Frage, ob es gut sei, am Klavier zu arbeiten, geantwortet: 'Die einen komponieren am Klavier, die anderen ohne. Und Sie werden eben am Klavier komponieren.' Von einem starken Bedürfnis nach unmittelbarer Berührung mit dem Instrument getrieben, komponierte Strawinsky bekanntlich sein ganzes Leben lang am Klavier.

In Ustilug, fern von jedem geistigen Zentrum, lebte die allerdings schon zahlreiche Familie gezwungenermassen ganz für sich. Ich erinnere mich nur an ein einziges neues Gesicht, dasjenige von Stefan Mitussow, einem guten Freund meines Vaters, der mit ihm das Libretto der *Nachtigall* abgefasst hatte. In Ustilug legte Strawinsky im Frühjahr 1910 die letzte Hand an die Partitur des *Feuervogel*. Ustilug bot dem Komponisten, nach seinen eigenen Worten, die ideale Abgeschiedenheit zum Komponieren.

Auf diesen Besitzungen, mitten in einer vorwiegend ländlichen Gegend, lebten viele Juden, alle in sehr bescheidenen Verhältnissen. Zur Erntezeit sah man sie in den umliegenden Obstgärten mit ihren grossen Zelten. Eines Tages klingelte eine schöne, lächelnde Raïssa an der Tür. Ich sehe noch, wie meine Mutter ihr öffnet und ich mich – oh Verblüffung! – den aufgesperrten Schnäbeln zweier Hühner mit starren Augen und aneinandergebundenen Füssen gegenübersehe: sie kam, um ihr Geflügel zu verkaufen. Meine Überraschung erreichte ihren Höhepunkt, als ich den Kopf hob und die seltene Haartracht der jungen Frau erblickte, eine Art Haube mit daraufgemalten roten Haaren. Ich ruhte nicht eher, als bis mein Vater mir erklärte, dass die jüdischen Frauen, zumindest in dieser Gegend, sich zu ihrem Hochzeitstag den Kopf schoren, und dass diejenigen, die sich keine richtige Perücke leisten konnten, sich damit begnügten, sorgfältig auf eine Leinenhaube falsche Haare mit dem Scheitel in der Mitte zu malen.

Gegen Ende der schönen Jahreszeit lösten die Reisevorbereitungen alljährlich bei der Familie ein allgemeines Durcheinander aus. Eltern, Grossmütter, Njanjas und Gouvernanten schnallen die Koffer zu und verschnüren die japanischen Körbe, nicht zu vergessen die denkwürdigen Hutschachteln – den heutigen Kindern unbekannt -, die die Jahrhundertwende unmässig gross hatte werden lassen. Dann versammelt Igor seine Leute. Schweigen. Ein uralter russicher Brauch verlangt, dass, wenn man einen Ort verlässt, zu dem man zurückkehren will, die ganze Familie sich im Augenblick der Abreise hinsetzt – 'prissest' –, sich einige Sekunden sammelt und sich beim Aufstehen bekreuzigt. Diese Sitte wurde im damaligen Russland überall eingehalten, und meine Eltern fügten sich ihr gern. Wir Kleinen empfanden trotz unserer Aufregung diese kurzen Augenblicke als etwas sehr Feierliches . . . aber sehr Langes!

Schon türmen sich auf der Vordertreppe Kisten und Koffer. Man nimmt in den Wagen Platz. Die Pferde schnauben und wiehern. Ein Peitschenknall, das Zeichen zur Abfahrt, und . . . leb wohl Ustilug, bis zum nächsten Jahr! Nach mehrstündigem Geschüttel Wladimir-Wolhynsk, dann abends Kowel. In der nächtlichen Stille, unter dem Sternenhimmel, hallen unsere Schritte auf den hölzernen Gehsteigen der kleinen Stadt wider: ich fürchte mich ein wenig, doch die Hand meines Vaters, die die meine hält, beruhigt mich. Im Hotel bestäubt unsere Mutter unser Bettzeug sorgfältig mit einem gelben Pulver, 'um die Flöhe zu vertreiben'; das gehörte zu unseren Reisevergnügen. Tags darauf der kleine Bahnhof in der prickelnden Morgenfrühe, der keuchende Zug bis nach Warschau. Dort, während wir auf den Schnellzug nach Berlin warteten, assen wir in jenem Bahnhofsrestaurant, in dessen Mitte ein riesiger verchromter Samowar in Form einer Lokomotive emporragte und seine Dampfwolken ausstiess; er fesselte meine Blicke. Auf dem Bahnsteig zählen Vater und Mutter immer wieder die Gepäcksstücke, während alles sich in den gepolsterten Abteilen des internationalen Expresszugs mit dem tressengeschmückten Personal verteilt.

Vierundzwanzig Stunden in Berlin. Höhepunkt dieses Tages in der deutschen Hauptstadt war immer ein herrlicher Besuch im Tiergarten, und ein anderer, nicht minder herrlicher in der Spielzeugabteilung eines Warenhauses. Dort kaufte man mir nach langer Probe, zu meinem grossen Stolz, meinen ersten Matrosenanzug. Mein Vater probiert gegen die Vorschriften der Hygiene nacheinander mehrere Pfeifen aus, zur grossen Verwirrung meiner Mutter, aber zu meiner Freude – wenngleich ich ein bisschen verlegen war, da die Verkäuferinnen uns zusahen –, und verblieb bei der Schrillsten, die er wie einen Orden an meinen neuen Anzug

heftete. An jenem Tag geriet plötzlich der ganze Laden in grosse Bewegung. Draussen war eine Hupe mit besonderem Klang ertönt. Alles stürzte zu Türen und Fenstern, und mein Vater hob mich auf seine Schultern, damit auch ich einen sehr ernsten Herrn in einem grossen weissen Kabriolett sehen konnte, der grüssend vorbeifuhr: der Kaiser.

Der wachsende Ruhm des damals sehr jungen Komponisten Igor Strawinsky liess schon zu seiner Begrüssung die gesamte Leitung des Russischen Musikverlags herbeieilen, der in Berlin seinen Sitz hatte, und das bedeutete allemal für uns Kinder die Verteilung von Berliner Zuckerwerk.

Station Paris. Übernachtung im Hotel d'Egypte in der rue des Pyramides. Die feierliche Standuhr hoch oben auf dem Kamin, aus schwarzem Marmor, mit ihrem vergoldeten Zifferblatt und den beiden Messingsphinxen tickte so laut, dass sie schliesslich über die Erregung des kleinen Reisenden die Oberhand gewann und ich endlich, -welch ein Privileg!- im Bett meiner Eltern einschlief.

Und wieder im Zug. Endlich La Baule! Nach der endlosen Reise liess es sich mein Vater, kaum angelangt, nicht nehmen, auf der Stelle seinen Sohn an das weite Meer zu führen und ihn zum ersten Mal Salzwasser schmecken zu lassen. Vetter, Kusine und Schwesterchen wurden einer solchen Einweihung nicht teilhaftig. Sie waren bei den Grossen geblieben, die die Koffer auspackten. Ich höre noch am Strand den Ruf des Waffelverkäufers: 'Kauft Waffeln, die feinen, die schmecken euren Kleinen!'. Das Quartier, das für Ende des Sommers gemietet wurde, war ein schokoladenfarbenes Chalet mitten in den Pinien. Dort komponierte mein Vater seine *Zwei Gedichte von Verlaine* für Bariton und Klavier, seinem Bruder Guri gewidmet, der Sänger war wie der Vater. Unser Onkel war damals bei uns in La Baule. Nach einigen Wochen kam die Familie in die Schweiz, und am 23. September 1910 schenkte meine Mutter in Lausanne ihrem dritten Kinde, meinen Bruder Svjatoslav-Sulima, das Leben.

Der Winter wurde in Beaulieu-sur-Mer verbracht. Eine Wohnung im ersten Stockwerk; im Erdgeschoss, was für ein Glück!, eine Konditorei: wir essen gezuckerte Veilchen und Mimosen. Und während mein Vater an *Petruschka* arbeitet und die ausgelassenen Volksszenen der Karnevalswoche komponiert – die sich bekanntlich in Petersburg vor dem Hintergrund einer nordischen Winterdämmerung abspielen-, ziehen unter seinen Fenstern, bei strahlender Mittelmeersonne, die Masken des Karnevals von Beaulieu vorbei. Am Abend nimmt mein Vater, Mutter und Tanten zum Umzug mit, und tags darauf sammeln meine Schwester und ich, mit Vetter und Kusine, auf allen Vieren in der ganzen Wohnung bunte Konfetti auf.

Immer noch in Beaulieu: vor mir zwei riesige und gold-glitzernde Messgewänder; Weihrauchwolken füllen das Esszimmer; ein grosses Kupferbecken voll Wasser, viel Gesang, und in meinen Händen eine grosse brennende Kerze. Alles scheint mir so schön! Es ist die Taufe unseres Brüderchens. Vater und Mutter haben stets die grösste Ehrfurcht vor dem Heiligen gehabt, vor den Riten und Überlieferungen der orthodoxen Kirche. Mit den Jahren wurde ihr Glaube immer tiefer, und mein Vater, der selbst wegen der äusseren Umstände die Religion später nicht ausübte, hielt nichts destoweniger an einem unerschütterlichen Glauben fest.

Bald, gegen Ende des Frühjahrs, weilt mein Vater kurze Zeit in Rom, wo er *Petrouschka* beendet, kehrt dann zu seiner Familie nach Beaulieu zurück, von wo man sich wieder gemeinsam nach Russland aufmacht, in den schönen ukrainischen Sommer in Ustilug, mit seinen saftigen Früchten und seinen, nach Ananas schmeckenden, weissen Erdbeeren. Noch ein kleines Kind mehr . . . noch eine Nurse!

Strawinsky entwirft in jenen Tagen eine Kantate für Männer-chor und Orchester: *Der Sternenkönig*, Claude Debussy gewidmet, und komponiert ein Diptychon für Gesang: *Zwei Gedichte von Balmont*, das *Vergissmeinnicht* und die *Taube*, das eine seiner Mutter, das andere seiner Schwägerin Ludmilla Beljankin gewidmet; aber vor allem beginnt er die Arbeit am *Frühlingsopfer*, wobei er eine Idee wiederaufnimmt, die ihn schon lange vor *Petruschka* verfolgt hatte.

Der erste Herbststreif vertreibt uns alle wieder; diesmal an die Ufer des Genfer Sees, in die Schweiz, nach Clarens, in die Pension des Tilleuls.

Mein Vater wusste seinen vielen vorläufigen Wohnsitzen immer etwas nahezu Endgültiges zu verleihen und sich die für sein Schaffen unerlässliche Abgeschiedenheit zu sichern. Sein ganzes Leben lang verbreitete er überall um sich seine eigene Atmosphäre. Das unpersönlichste Hotelzimmer wurde von seiner Persönlichkeit geprägt, ja gezeichnet. Die Wände gaben dann Aufschluss darüber, was ihn jeweils faszinierte, vom edelsten Werk der Antike bis zum volkstümlichen Stich. Aber in jenen Jahren sind es die japanischen Holzschnitte, die den Ehrenplatz einnehmen, eine Kunst, die die europäische Elite mit Begeisterung entdeckte und wiederentdeckte; und Strawinsky komponiert die *Drei Japanischen Gedichte* für hohe Stimme und Klavier: *Akahito* für Maurice Delage, *Masatsumi* für Florent Schmitt und *Zarajoki* für Maurice Ravel.

Auf das schmiedeeiserne Balkongitter vor unseren Fenstern im Hôtel du Châtelard (1913) gestützt, sehe ich noch neben meinem Vater einen adretten kleinen Herrn mit glühenden Augen, dichten Brauen und schönem, silbergrauem Haar. Ich höre sie noch, wie sie beide fünf, zehn, fünfzehnmal den Amseln im Garten eine kurze Phrase zupfiffen, auf welche diese zu meiner kindlichen Freude, schliesslich antworteten. Der kleine Herr war niemand anderer als Maurice Ravel.

Ihre gemeinsame Vorliebe für die japanische Kunst und ihre ästhetischen Bestrebungen, soweit sie sich damals deckten, nährten die Freundschaft zwischen Ravel und Strawinsky. Die beiden Musiker lebten während einiger Wochen als Nachbarn und sahen sich täglich. Nur die Eisenbahnschienen trennten das Hôtel des Crêtes, wo der französische Komponist wohnte, vom heute abgeris-senen Hôtel du Châtelard, wo der russische Komponist mit seiner Familie lebte. Wenn dieser in Clarens ein Klima suchte, das der Gesundheit seiner jungen Frau zuträglich war, fand Ravel, von seiner Mutter begleitet, in dieser Gegend die Wiege seiner Familie. Sollte diese Stätte dazu ausersehen sein, Musiker aufzunehmen? Mendel-sohn weilte lange hier, Tschaikowsky komponierte hier *Die Jungfrau von Orleans*, und in unseren Tagen verbrachte hier Paul Hindemith seine letzten Lebensjahre.

Strawinsky, seinerseits, beendet hier, im Hôtel du Châtelard, die Arbeit am *Frühlingsopfer*.

Verweilen wir dabei. Muss man nicht die verblüffende schöp-ferische Vitalität des dreissigjährigen jungen Musikers bewundern? Sollte er nicht in den drei Jahren 1910 bis 1913 die drei Meisterwerke zustande bringen, die ihn auf den Gipfel des Ruhmes hoben: *Feuervogel*, *Petruschka*, *Frühlingsopfer*. Und das, indem er, wie wir gesehen haben, als wahrer Patriarch die Pflichten für eine Familie voll wahrnahm, die in ständigem Wanderzustand lebte. Und er brachte es fertig, dazu noch zahlreiche persönliche Reisen zu unternehmen; fuhr er nicht ständig zu Diagilev und seiner Truppe nach Paris, Rom, Bayreuth . . . ? Die aufsehenerregende Premiere des *Frühlingsopfers* fand bekanntlich am 29. Mai 1913 im Théâtre des Champs-Elysées in Paris statt. Ein paar Tage später schien ein Typhusfieber, das ihn in der französischen Hauptstadt befallen hatte und dort behandelt wurde, eine dramatische Wendung nehmen zu wollen, und beunruhigte Verwandte und Freunde des Komponisten, die um sein Leben bangten.

Den Sommer verbringt die Familie wieder, wie immer, in Ustilug. Der Genesende komponierte hier, 'um sich zu unterhalten', die *Erinnerung an meine Kindheit*, drei kleine Stücke für Gesang und Klavier, die er seinen drei Kindern, Theodor, Ludmilla und Svjatoslav-Sulima widmete, und die er zwanzig Jahre später für eine kleine Instrumentalgruppe transkribierte.

Im Herbst zurück nach Clarens. Wer aber konnte ahnen, dass Russland diesmal für immer verlassen und Ustilug auf ewig verloren war?

Am 15. Januar 1914 erblickte unsere Schwester Milena, viertes und letztes Kind unserer Eltern, in Lausanne das Licht der Welt. Unsere Mutter, durch die Niederkunft erschöpft, wurde zu einem längeren Aufenthalt in die Berge nach Leysin geschickt, wohin ihr Gatte sie begleitete, was von jener Besorgtheit und Aufmerksamkeit zeugt, die ihn stets kennzeichnete, wenn es um die Gesundheit der Seinen ging. In Leysin sollte zwischen meinen Eltern und Jean Cocteau eine bleibende, echte Freundschaft entstehen; echt, weil sie trotz zahlreicher Unstimmigkeiten, Ärgernisse und sogar Trübungen nie verleugnet wurde und unweigerlich eines Tages zu einer engen Zusammenarbeit an einem grossen Bühnenwerk führte, dem *Oedipus Rex* aus dem Jahre 1926.

Als meine Eltern sich 1914 entschlossen, nicht nach festem Brauch für den Sommer nach Russland zurückzukehren, sondern in der Schweizer Höhe zu bleiben, ahnten sie nicht im entferntesten die für den Rest ihres Lebens bestimmenden Folgen dieses Entschlusses, der einzig aus vorübergehenden gesundheitlichen Sorgen entsprungen war. Denn nach Leysin, und nachdem die ganze Familie in den kleinen Sommerkurort Salvan im Wallis in die Pension Bel-Air übergesiedelt war, brach der Erste Weltkrieg aus. Da mein Vater nicht eingezogen werden konnte, brauchte er nicht in seine Heimat zurückzukehren. Er sollte den heimatlichen Boden erst achtundvierzig Jahre später wiedersehen, nach seinem achtzigsten Geburtstag.

Am 26. Mai fand endlich in Paris die Premiere der *Nachtigall* statt, eines schon 1908 in Petersburg begonnenen Werkes, das

lange unvollendet geblieben war. In Salvan schmückten die Entwürfe für die Bühnenbilder dieser Oper, die ihr Schöpfer Alexandre Benois seinem Freunde Igor Strawinsky geschenkt hatte, das Arbeitszimmer meines Vaters. Hier komponierte er *Pribautki*, mit der Stimme seines Bruders Guri im Sinne, und *Drei Stücke für Streichquartett*.

Hier erkannte ich auch einestages an der finsteren und besorgten Miene meiner Eltern, dass etwas sehr Schlimmes vorging. 'Man sagt, es wird Krieg geben', erklärte mir bestürzt meine Grossmutter, die damals bei uns war. Wenige Tage später wurde die neutrale Schweizer Armee mobilisiert, und täglich fanden Schiessübungen auf der Wiese vor unserer Pension statt. Meine kleinen Spielkameraden und ich hatten bald ein Spiel mit den Patronenhülsen, die wir stolz auflasen, herausgefunden. Zur Essenszeit, am Gästetisch, wandte mein Vater allerlei kleine Listen an, um den aufdringlichen Theorien einer berühmten und berüchtigten Theosophin zu entgehen . . . und schärfte uns ein, wir dürften nicht die köstlichen Lebkuchen mit Marmelade annehmen, die sie uns andauernd anbieten wollte!

Im Herbst geht es wieder nach Clarens herunter, diesmal nicht mehr ins Hotel, sondern in eine Villa, als Untermieter von Ernest Ansermet. Man weiss, welch enges Band sich damals zwischen dem Komponisten und dem Dirigenten knüpfte, und welch bedeutende Rolle Ansermet später bei der weltweiten Verbreitung der ersten Werke Strawinskys spielen sollte. In dieser gewöhnlichen, kleinen Villa La Pervenche, begann mein Vater an einer seiner wichtigsten Partituren zu arbeiten, an der *Hochzeit*. Immer wieder hinausgeschoben, wurde die Arbeit im Laufe der folgenden Jahre mehrmals wiederaufgenommen, während der Komponist viele andere Werke zu Ende führte: *Reinecke Fuchs*, *Die Geschichte vom Soldaten*, *Ragtime*, *Pulcinella*, *Concertino*, *Bläsersymphonien*, *Mawra* und einige minder bedeutende Werke. Die endgültige Instrumentierung der *Hochzeit* wurde erst neun Jahre später festgelegt.

So sind wir denn im Herbst 1914 in Clarens. In diese Zeit fällt die traurige Trennung von meiner Grossmutter, die beschlossen hatte, wieder in unsere Heimat im Kriegszustand zurückzukehren. Seit mehr als zehn Jahren verwitwet, lebte sie bald in ihrer Wohnung in Petersburg, die sie mit Guri, ihrem Jüngsten, teilte, bald in unserer Familie, die sie während einiger Wochen oder Monate begleitete, sei es nach Ustilug, in die Schweiz oder nach Frankreich

... Nun hatte sich der unerschrockene Onkel Guri als Freiwilliger an die Balkanfront gemeldet, und sie wollte ihm näher sein. Roman, ihren Ältesten, hatte sie verloren. Juri und Igor waren verheiratet und hatten Familie. Auf ihren Jüngsten hatte sie die ganze Zärtlichkeit ihres Mutterherzens übertragen. Tapfer begab sie sich also allein, mitten im Krieg, auf die lange, gefahrvolle Reise, die sie über die gefährlichen Wasser der Dardanellen von der Schweiz nach Russland führte. Später in Petersburg, das zu Leningrad geworden war, erlebte sie die ganze Revolution und die harten Jahre, die darauf folgten. Die Treuen Freunde ihrer Söhne fanden, um sie zu schützen, und damit sie in ihrer Wohnung bleiben konnte, einen glücklichen und listigen Ausweg: es gelang ihnen, sie zur Hüterin der Bibliothek ihres eigenen Gatten zu machen, die das neue Regime gerade verstaatlicht hatte.

Nachdem unsere Grossmutter uns verlassen hatte, wohnte unsere Familie während eines kurzen winterlichen Zwischenspiels in Château-d'Oex in den Waadtländer Alpen, im Hotel Victoria (1914–1915). Ist es nicht ein Wunder, dass unsere Eltern es verstanden, inmitten eines so bewegten Lebens für ihre Kinder eine wahre, friedliche Familienatmosphäre zu schaffen und zu bewahren? Obwohl Igor sich über Kleinigkeiten aufregen konnte, war er ein besorgter Vater, einmal so nah und von so wohltuender, warmer Menschlichkeit und dann wieder unnahbar, wenn er in die geheime Welt des Schaffens versenkt war ... Zu seiner Seite Katharina, die Gattin, die Mutter, sanft, von ausserordentlicher seelischer Grosszügigkeit, sich ganz und gar aufopfernd, aber immer gegenwärtig ...

Aber das Wanderleben, das unsere Familie während dieser ersten sieben Jahre meiner Kindheit geführt hatte, sollte bald ein Ende nehmen. Die Ausdehnung des Krieges über die ganze Welt zwang nun unsere Eltern, eine feste Niederlassung in der Schweiz ins Auge zu fassen. Das Schulproblem für die heranwachsende Kinderschar brachte sie auch zu einem derartigen Entschluss. Feste Freundschaften verbanden meinen Vater schon mit diesem Boden der französischen Schweiz, die bis 1920 seine Zufluchtsstätte bleiben sollte. In der Umgebung von Lausanne, am Genfer See, wählen Igor und Katharina die reizende kleine Stadt Morges, und im Frühjahr 1915 mieten sie da in der Avenue des Pâquis die Villa Rogivue.

Von jener Zeit an begann sich nicht nur das väterliche Arbeitszimmer, sondern auch das ganze Haus mit Nippsachen und Möbeln zu füllen, die man bei den Antiquitätenhändlern und Trödlern der Umgebung aufgestöbert hatte; glückliche Zeit, wo man noch überraschende Funde machen konnte! Diese Gegenstände wurden später, nachdem sie die Familie in ihre verschiedenen Wohnungen begleitet hatten, für uns zu Erinnerungsstücken, von denen einige zu meiner grossen Freude seit mehr als dreissig Jahren bei mir stehen. Der Schweizer Tisch aus dem 18. Jahrhundert mit der dicken, dunklen Birnbaumplatte (er war schon in Clarens gekauft worden), auf dem so viele Partituren, vom *Frühlingsopfer* bis zum *Dumbarton Oaks Concerto*, entstanden ... der grosse Schrank mit der naiv-bunten Bemalung, in dem mein Vater seine Manuskripte einordnete ... die aus Italien mitgebrachten, neapolitanischen Gouaschen ...

In Morges verschwinden die japanischen Holzschnitte von den Wänden der Villa Rogivue. Sie werden durch die kraftvollen Entwürfe Larijonows für den *Reinecke Fuchs* und durch die hübschen Aquarelle mit den kräftigen Farben, die meine Mutter damals als Illustration zum Text der *Hochzeit* malte, ersetzt. Hatte sie nicht mit ihrer grossen Zeichenbegabung als junges Mädchen mit ihren Kusinen einige Monate an der Academie Colarossi in Paris gearbeitet ...

Was für uns bis dahin nur mehr oder weniger geheimnisvolle Namen gewesen waren, die die Erwachsenen aussprachen, oder höchstens Gestalten, die wir flüchtig in den Hotelkorridoren erblickt hatten, werden nun allmählich Wirklichkeit. Unsere kindlichen Zuneigungen werden wählerisch. So wird Diagilev bald 'Onkel Sergej' mit den vertrauenerweckenden dicken Backen. Wir stürzten ihm entgegen, kletterten auf seine Knie, da wir wussten, dass seine Taschen immer voller Bonbons für uns waren. Viel später erst erzählte mir mein Vater, dass er eine Geheimtasche hatte, allein für die zahlreichen Amulette, von denen sich dieser abergläubischste aller Menschen nie trennte. Nijinsky hingegen, schmächtig und mit verlorenem Blick, liess uns kalt, obwohl uns unsere Mutter erklärt hatte, dieser Herr sei der grösste Tänzer der Welt, und wenn er springe, scheine er zu fliegen ... Stundenlang schloss sich mein Vater mit ihnen in sein Arbeitszimmer ein, und durch die Tür drangen donnernde Akkorde zu uns, unterbrochen von plötzlichen Ausrufen, die manchmal so laut waren, dass sie uns Angst machten. 'Dürfen sie denn Papa schelten?' fragte ängstlich meine Schwester Mika (Ludmilla). Und gross war unsere Erleichterung und unser

Staunen, wenn die drei Grossen mit einem Lächeln auf den Lippen heraustraten.

Diagilev, Nijinsky, Massin, Larjonov, Gontscharowa, Prokofjev und ein paar andere, das war die Welt des Russischen Balletts; es waren Freundschaften, die in Russland entstanden waren. Dieser Gruppe von Freunden können wir auch noch den Chorleiter Basil Kibaltchitch anschliessen. Alle erlitten sie jetzt, wie meine Eltern, gezwungenermassen das gemeinsame Los der Emigranten. In Morges wurden neue Freundschaften geknüpft, die dann im Leben meines Vaters eine ebenso wichtige Rolle spielten. Ernest Ansermet, der Schriftsteller C.F.Ramuz, die Maler René Auberjonois, Henri Bischoff, Jean Morax und dessen Bruder, der Dramatiker René Morax, Alexandre Cingria, ein weiterer Maler und dessen Bruder Charles-Albert Cingria, dieser grosse, allzu wenig bekannte Dichter . . . Sie bildeten den Mittelpunkt eines ganzen Kreises von Freunden, die meine Eltern jederzeit gern in ihrem stets offenen Haus, an ihrem stets gedeckten Tisch empfingen. Wenn es auch damals an Sorgen nicht fehlte, die warme russische Gastfreundschaft kam doch zu ihrem Recht. Zahllos waren die Freunde, die die Strawinskys in Morges beherbergten.

Mein Gedächtnis bewahrt und vermischt mit Glücksempfinden und Rührung unsere glitzernden Weihnachtsfeiern und unsere russischen Ostern, und besonders jenes Neujahrsfest, an dem Vater und Mutter sich zu unserer Belustigung verkleideten. Das Familienoberhaupt erschien als Maler-Dilettant, mit Rembrandt-Mütze, Lavalliere-Krawatte, Staffelei auf der Schulter, Palette und Pinsel in der Hand . . .

Für uns Kinder verläuft das Leben im Schulrhythmus. Zu Hause geht man morgens auf Zehenspitzen . . . Strawinsky komponiert. Da fängt doch das Zimmermädchen, das Ruhegebot vergessend, zu singen oder gar die Köchin zu pfeifen an! Mehr braucht es nicht, um einen Zornesausbruch des Komponisten hervorzurufen. Und meine Mutter muss ihre ganze Diplomatie aufwenden, um ihren Gatten zu beruhigen . . . und ihre Angestellten zu behalten! Nachmittags dagegen ist die Stimmung entspannt. Meistens orchestriert mein Vater, während zu seiner Seite in diesen ruhigen Stunden meine Mutter Partituren und Klavierauszüge abschreibt, bis wir aus der Schule zurückkommen. Jetzt beginnt die Russisch-Stunde. Während ich nach dem Diktat der Mutter schreibe oder ihr irgendeine Stelle vorlese, sehe ich noch das kleine Gerät, mit dem sie flink die Lieblingszigaretten meines Vaters herstellte, aus einem besonderen Tabak, der das ganze Haus mit seinem Duft erfüllt. Er rauchte sie aus einer langen, leicht gebogenen Zigarettenspitze, aus 'sehr, sehr kostbarem Albatrosschnabel!', wie man uns sagte. Mit unseren Eltern haben wir Kinder immer russisch gesprochen; in der Schule und unter uns französisch; deutsch mit den Gouvernanten.

Wenn das Leben für die Seinen nun sesshaft geworden war, mein Vater gab das Reisen nicht auf. An Gelegenheiten dazu fehlte es im Zusammenhang mit dem Russischen Ballett nicht, obwohl die Reisemöglichkeiten wegen der Ausbreitung der Feindseligkeiten beschränkt waren. Die Freundschaft zwischen Strawinsky und Diagilev war echt, und gross die gegenseitige Bewunderung. Dennoch machte sich mein Vater kaum Illusionen über die 'Versuchungen', die diese Umgebung für ihn darstellte. Schon in einem Brief vom 14.X.1912 aus Ustilug an seinen Freund Maurice Delage steht unter anderem über seine Beziehungen zum Russischen Ballett dies erstaunliche Bekenntnis: '. . . der Ruhm und das Geld, dessen Versuchungen mich im Innersten zerfressen . . .'. Man ersieht daraus auch, dass er sich keine Illusionen über die verlogene Atmosphäre und die Intrigen hinter den Kulissen der berühmten Truppe und über den Snobismus, der in ihr herrschte, machte. Doch so ist das Leben. Sein tiefgründiges Wesen und seine Kunst stellten von Anfang an doppelte und widersprüchliche Anforderungen an Strawinsky. War es nicht derselbe Mann, der von der ausserordentlichsten Lebenskraft übersprudelte, und der nach aussen gewandt war, weniger weil es die Verbreitung seiner Werke verlangte, als wegen eines echten Bedürfnisses nach direktem Kontakt mit dem Hörer-Publikum, – und der zugleich in seinem Familienleben die ideale Atmosphäre fand, um an diesem Werk zu arbeiten? Daraus ergab sich ein echtes, inniges Familienleben, jedoch mit der ständigen Abwechslung durch seine Reisen, auf denen er hier und dort Diagilev und seine Truppe traf, dann später durch seine Konzerttourneen. Dieses Leben auf zwei Ebenen dauerte bis zum Winter 1938–1939, in dessen Verlauf er innerhalb von sechs tragischen Monaten nacheinander seine Tochter Ludmilla, seine Frau und seine Mutter verlor. Kein Heim mehr, die Familie löst sich auf . . . Jeder von uns geht seiner Wege. Mein Vater geht den seinen, indem er 1940 in den Vereinigten Staaten Vera Sudeïkin, geborene de Bosset, heiratet.

Aber kehren wir nach Morges in die Jahre 1915–1916 zurück. Mit unserer Mutter erwarteten wir mit grösster Ungeduld die Rückkehr unseres reisenden Vaters – sei es aus Rom, aus Madrid oder aus Paris. Von seinen Tourneen brachte er uns immer irgendein unerwartetes Geschenk mit, so die Schallplatte eines Stierkampfes, auf der die Trompetenstösse, die Olé-Rufe der Menge und vor allem das Brüllen des Stiers uns in Atem hielt, während Vater, der bei schmächtigem Körperbau doch überaus muskulös war, uns die Bewegungen des Toreros mit der stets auf seinem Sofa liegenden roten Decke vormachte. In Erinnerung an seine erste Berührung mit Spanien komponierte Strawinsky bald ein Stück für Pianola mit dem Titel *Madrid*. In einer Instrumentalfassung baute er es später in seine *Vier Etüden für Orchester* ein. Und noch später schrieb der ausgezeichnete Pianist, zu dem sich sein eigener Sohn Sulima entwickelt hatte, dieses *Madrid* unserer Kindheit für zwei Klaviere um.

Und dann gibt es noch die 'Española' aus den *Fünf leichten Stücken*, die mich (genau wie die *Drei leichten Stücke*) unweigerlich an unsere erste Berührung mit dem Klavier erinnern, sozusagen an die ersten Schritte der Kinderfinger auf der Tastatur, ans erste Notenlesen auf der Notenlinie; und auch an das schöne Waschblau der Wände im väterlichen Arbeitszimmer, wo sich jeder von uns, der Reihe nach, zwanzig Minuten ans Klavier setzte, auf den Klavierstuhl, der immer hoch genug eingestellt war, dass wir das Pedal nicht erreichen konnten – grausame Versuchung! Unser Lehrer? Der Vater selbst, Igor Strawinsky, der da bei seinen kleinen Schülern eine erstaunliche Geduld bewies, oder vielmehr, glaube ich, – ich bin sogar sicher – eine natürliche Ungeduld bezwang. Finden wir nicht dieselbe bezwungene Ungeduld in seinem Umgang mit den Orchestermusikern wieder, bei jenem Manne, der die Ungeduld in Person war?

Eines Tages kam mein Vater von Einkäufen in Genf zurück, voll Freude darüber, dass er eine ungarische Zimbel aufgetrieben hatte, ein seltenes Instrument, von dem er seit einiger Zeit träumte, und das er in den *Reinecke Fuchs* einfügen wollte, an dem er arbeitete. Immer dieses Bedürfnis nach unmittelbarer Berührung mit dem Instrument. Ich sehe noch vor mir, wie dieser unbekannte Gegenstand ins Haus kommt. Kaum im Hof ausgepackt – wo unser Vater uns darauf vorspielte – entzückte uns dies es Erwachsenen-Spielzeug, und jeder durfte es der Reihe nach ausprobieren. Sobald es aber im väterlichen Arbeitszimmer den Platz eingenommen hatte, der ihm zugedacht war, durfte es nicht mehr berührt werden! Zur Zeit der *Geschichte vom Soldaten* erwarb er so eine ganze Reihe von Schlaginstrumenten. Die Pauke, der Bemalung nach zu schliessen – abwechselnd grüne und weisse Dreiecke – konnte nur irgendeiner Waadtländer Dorfkapelle entstammen.

Ende 1915, genau gesagt am 20. Dezember, veranstaltete Sergej Diagilev zugunsten des Internationalen Roten Kreuzes in Genf (der Wiege dieser Institution) einen grossen Galaabend. Ein denkwürdiges Datum für Igor Strawinsky; an jenem Abend dirigierte er zum ersten Mal öffentlich. Auf dem Programm steht unter seiner Leitung eine symphonische Suite aus dem *Feuervogel*; unter der Leitung Ernest Ansermets das Ballet *Karneval* nach Schumann und *Nachtsonne* von Rimsky-Korsakov. Wie gross war meine Überraschung, meine Freude und mein Stolz, als meine Eltern mir sagten, sie würden mich ins Theater mitnehmen. Die weit geöffneten Augen des mit visueller Phantasie begabten Jungen, der ich sein sollte, nahmen begierig alles auf: Vorhang, Bühne, Zuschauerraum, Leuchter, das Rot, das Gold; den Zuschauerraum im Dunkeln, die Bühne im Rampenlicht, und neben mir in der Proszeniumsloge, so hübsch in ihrem blassblauen Kleid, meine Mutter. Und dann der Orchesterraum, das grosse schwarze Loch mit den kleinen Lichtern, aus dem unter Beifall plötzlich beweglich und leicht die Gestalt meines Vaters auftauchte. Ein Sprung, und er steht am Pult. Er verneigt sich tief, dreht sich um, und gemessen und mit Bedacht zerbricht er den Stab. Der Atem stockte mir . . . Der Stab war ihm einfach zu lang. Dann Monsieur Ansermet mit dem so schwarzen Bart auf der weissen Hemdbrust. In der Pause das glänzende und glatte Parkett, die Herren im Frack, die nach Parfum riechenden Damen, und die Genfer Gendarmen in vollem Staat mit Zweispitz, Schulterklappen, Tressen, Wehrgehängen und weissen Handschuhen . . . die funkelnden Leuchter, die unendlich aus den riesigen Spiegeln des Foyers widerstrahlten . . . Und wie sollte ich die grosse Dame ganz in Weiss vergessen, die in unserer Loge erschien, und die eben zu Beginn der Darbietung vor dem Vorhang die russische Nationalhymne 'Gott erhalte uns den Zaren' gesungen hatte? Felia Litvin, die einst zu den Berühmtheiten der kaiserlichen Oper in Petersburg zählte, neigte sich zu mir, drückte mich an ihren füllingen Busen und flüsterte mir auf russisch ins Ohr: 'Weisst du, Theodorchen, als du noch nicht auf der Welt warst, habe ich mit dem grossen Theodor, deinem Grossvater gesungen'. Ich rieche noch den merkwürdigen Vanilleduft der Schminke auf ihrem Gesicht. Ich war ein wenig eingeschüchtert . . . Dann zum Schluss, vor dem Vorhang, Onkel Sergej, der sich verbeugte und die hübschen Tänzerinnen bei der Hand hielt. Wieviel Aufregungen, wieviel neue Eindrücke! Wunderbare Aufnahmefähigkeit eines kleinen Menschen, der zum ersten Mal einer wahren Traum- und Wunderwelt begegnet, die plötzlich Wirklichkeit geworden ist und sich sogleich auf ewig seinem Gedächtnis einprägt.

In Morges, unter dem väterlichen Dach, hatten wir Familienzuwachs bekommen durch unsere liebe alte Bertha Essert, die deutschen Ursprungs war, und die mein Vater trotz der Feindseligkeiten hatte 'heimholen' können. Sie war schon vor der Geburt Igors in die Familie Strawinsky gekommen und war die treue Njanja seiner Kindheit gewesen. Es gab nichts, womit sie nicht einst ihn und seine Brüder verwöhnt hatte und nun uns Kinder Igors verwöhnte. Doch was ist eigentlich genau eine Njanja? Es ist kein Zeugnis, kein Amt, nicht einmal das der Aufsicht, das sie manchmal übernimmt. Es ist sozusagen ein Status, den sie erwirbt. Es gab keine halbwegs begüterte russische Familie, die nicht ihre Njanja gehabt hätte, ein unentbehrliches Wesen für das seelische Wohl einer Familie, eine Art Grossmutterersatz, durch den sich jedoch niemand in den Schatten gestellt fühlte, denn sie verdrängte niemanden. Ganz im Gegenteil, eine Njanja ergänzte die traditionelle russische Familie, sie rundete sie gewissermassen ab. Eine Njanja erwirbt das Familienrecht, wie man das Bürgerrecht erwirbt, durch stete Hingabe an die gemeinsame Sache. Sie beschliesst ihre Tage geachtet und geliebt von einer, zwei oder gar drei Generationen. Einige Njanjas sind berühmt geblieben, wir denken an diejenige Puschkins, die der Dichter in unvergesslichen Versen besungen hat. Die liebe gute Bertha war unsere, so wie sie die unseres Vaters gewesen war, wir liebten sie wie eine richtige Grossmutter. Sie verschied unerwartet eines schönen Nachmittags im Frühjahr 1917. Grosse Aufregung herrschte im Haus, dann plötzlich grosse Stille. Man sprach leise, man ging auf Zehenspitzen. Unbekannte Männer gingen die Treppe hinauf und hinab. Ich sah zum ersten Mal, wie Vater und Mutter heisse Tränen vergossen, und wie enge Freunde meiner Eltern mit seltsamer Rücksicht begegneten . . . Ein lutherischer Pfarrer in langem schwarzem Umhang kam, und die traurige Ehrerbietung, die ihm mein Vater

bezeugte, beeindruckte mich . . . Es war das erste Mal, dass ich mich der geheimnisvollen Wirklichkeit des Todes gegenübersah. Doch war ich mir nicht schon kurz zuvor gewissermassen seiner Existenz bewusst geworden? War nicht auch die Njanja meiner Mutter und ihrer Schwester, Sophie Welsowsky – Baba Sonja –, wenn auch in der Ferne in Russland, bei den Beljankins verschieden? Ich kam aus der Schule zurück; ich fand Mama in Tränen und Papa, der sie mit grosser Zärtlichkeit tröstete. 'Baba Sonja ist tot, wir werden sie nicht wiedersehen . . .' Die liebe Baba Sonja, untrennbar verbunden mit unseren Erinnerungen aus der Zeit vor 1914 . . .

Die Villa Rogivue war sehr traurig geworden. Damals kam Mina Switalski als Gouvernante für die Älteren zu uns. Es dauerte nicht lange, bis sie unsere neue Njanja wurde; es war die so feinfühlige, unvergessliche Madubo, ein Spitzname, den ihr mein Bruder gab, als er sie sah, und der alsbald ihr Name für uns alle und für alle unsere Freunde wurde. Sie sollte Zeit ihres Lebens bei den einen oder den anderen von uns bleiben. Und wiegte sie nicht, als sie uns alle vier aufgezogen hatte, noch die kleine Katharina, die Tochter von Ludmilla, und den kleinen John, den Sohn von Sulima? Und nachdem sie mehr als vierzig Jahre bei den Strawinskys verbracht hatte, war es mir beschieden, dass sie in meiner Gegenwart ihren letzten Atemzug tat.

Im Sommer 1917, nach dem Hinscheiden Berthas, empfanden meine Eltern das Bedürfnis, die Umgebung zu wechseln. Immer noch ganz nach russischer Art übersiedelte der Hausstaat ins Gebirge, nach Les Diablerets in den Waadtländer Alpen. Dem Umzug voran das Klavier; dann Koffer und Pakete; der Hund Mouche und eine ganze Geflügelschar in Weidenkäfigen; Köchin, Zimmermädchen, Gouvernante, Madubo, Papa, Mama und ihre vier Kinder. Das Chalet Les Fougères nahm uns alle auf. Der Besitzer, ein braver Tischler im Ruhestand, liess 'den kauzigen russischen Herrn' sich in der ehemaligen Werkstatt einrichten. Sieht man nicht alsbald an den verwunderten Wänden dieses ungewohnten Arbeitszimmers die Photographien von den ausserordentlichen 'Plakatträgern' erscheinen, die Picasso für *Parade* entworfen hatte, ein Ballet von Eric Satie und Jean Cocteau, das Diagilev vor kurzem in Rom aufgeführt hatte? Dort arbeitete Strawinsky während des Sommers, an derselben Hobelbank wie der Handwerker, am letzten Bild der *Hochzeit*.

Durch das Glasfenster dieser Werkstatt erblickte ich einmal

ein noch unbekanntes Gesicht: ein Herr mit bleichem, flachem, rundem und glattem Gesicht und grosser Brille sprach in heftigem Ton mit meinem Vater. Dann spielten sie hinten im Garten unter einer Laube Karten. Nachdem der Herr, der in einen weiten Lodenumhang gehüllt war, zu dem kleinen Dorfbahnhof zurückbegleitet worden war, sagte uns unser Vater: 'Er war wütend, weil er die ganze Zeit verloren hat!'. Und dabei hatte man uns immer gesagt, dass man nie wütend werden dürfe, wenn man beim Spiel verliere! Der Verlierer des Nachmittags war André Gide. Wenn es Jahre später, 1933, zwischen Strawinsky und Gide für *Persephone* zu einer Zusammenarbeit kam, konnte sie, obwohl sie Anlass zu zahlreichen Begegnungen war, nicht zwei Naturen näherbringen, die ein Abgrund voneinander trennte.

Noch ein Besuch: der von Jacques Copeau, begleitet von seiner Tochter Mayenne, die wenig älter war als wir, und von deren langem, blondem Haar ich träumte ...

Das in jenem Sommer besonders schöne Wetter brachte meinen Vater oft dazu, auf unsere kleinen Ausflüge mitzukommen. Eines Tages, nachdem wir einen langen Nachmittag Himbeeren im Wald gepflückt hatten und jeder seinen Eimer voll mit der leichten, duftenden kleinen Frucht trug, kehrten wir fröhlich in die Fougères zurück. Ich höre noch meine Eltern sagen: 'Wirklich, was für ein herrlicher Tag!'. Genau in diesem Augenblick kam ein Telegraphenbote auf dem Fahrrad zu uns. Mein Vater las das Telegramm, gab es meiner Mutter. 'Onkel Guri ist gestorben', sagte sie. 'Weit weg von hier, an der rumänischen Front', fügte langsam mein Vater hinzu. Er ergriff die Hand meiner Mutter, schweigend kehrten wir nach Hause zurück. Die Blutsverwandtschaft zwischen dem Ehepaar Igor und Katharina Strawinsky – sie waren ja Geschwisterkinder – liess sie gleich stark Leid und Freud der Familie empfinden.

Wieder in Morges, sahen unsere Eltern sich unerwarteten Sorgen gegenüber: die Villa Rogivue, die wir seit Mai 1915 bewohnten, war eben überraschend von ihrem Besitzer verkauft worden. Man musste also wieder umziehen, und zwar schnell. Zum Glück fanden sie zwei Schritte weiter eine grosse und reizende Wohnung, place St Louis, in einem schönen Haus aus dem 18. Jahrhundert, Maison Bornand genannt. Wir Kinder mussten dem grossen Garten Lebewohl sagen, der seit mehr als zwei Jahren Zeuge unserer Spiele gewesen war.

Für Igor und Katharina begann nun ein langes, schmerzliches Leben ohne Kontakt mit der Heimat. Nach der Oktoberrevolution mussten sie einsehen, dass die Trennung leider endgültig war. Ein verständliches Heimweh erklärt wohl hinlänglich, warum Strawinsky damals so sehr für die russische Volkskunst schwärmte, deren unerschöpflichen Reichtum er liebevoll erforschte und auswertete. Diese Volkskunst lag ihm wahrhaft am Herzen. *Pribautki, Katzenwiegenlieder, Vier russische Lieder, Die Hochzeit, Reinecke Fuchs*, all diese Gesangswerke zeugen doch von einer Art schöpferischer Aneignung.

Hierher gehört die Zusammenarbeit meines Vaters mit C.F.Ramuz. Es ging Strawinsky weniger um eine Übersetzung seiner Texte als um eine französische Fassung, die nicht die Prosodie verfälschte, die er im Russischen hergestellt hatte. Nur eine dichterische Einfühlung wie die von Ramuz – weil sie sowohl menschlich, wie ästhetisch, mit der Strawinskys in Einklang stand – erlaubte es den beiden Freunden, wie durch ein Wunder, ein Unternehmen zuende zu führen, das ihnen hätte wahnwitzig erscheinen müssen: der Autor der französischen Fassung konnte ja kein Wort russisch! Aber diese Zusammenarbeit erwies sich für beide als denkbar befriedigend. Man braucht, um sich davon zu überzeugen, nur nachzulesen, was Strawinsky selbst in seiner *Chronik* sagt, und was Ramuz auf einigen meisterhaften Seiten seiner *Erinnerungen an Strawinsky* darüber schreibt.

Strawinsky hat sich wie Ramuz immer vor Theorien gehütet. Da sie beide so sehr aufs Konkrete bedacht waren, glitten ihre Gespräche über die Kunst nie ins Schulmässige ab. Die beiden Freunde sahen sich jetzt fast täglich. Früh morgens holten wir gern, wenn wir nicht in der Schule waren, Monsieur Ramuz vom Bahnhof ab, und erst mit dem letzten Abendzug kehrte er nach Lausanne heim.

Kommen wir jetzt zur wichtigsten Frucht der Verbindung Strawinsky-Ramuz: der *Geschichte vom Soldaten*. Der Text wurde diesmal ausschliesslich von Ramuz geschrieben, das Thema entstammte einem russischen Volksmärchen, das Strawinsky seinem Freund erzählte, und die ganze Geschichte wurde in ein imaginäres Waadtland versetzt. Hier eine kleine Nebenbemerkung: mein Vater erzählte gerne, wie er eines Nachts, 1918, als er an der *Geschichte vom Soldaten* arbeitete, im Traum eine schöne Zigeunerin vor der Türe ihres Wagens sitzen sah. Während sie ihrem Kind die Brust reichte, spielte die junge Frau auf einer Violine eine Tango-Melodie. 'Dies ist das einzige Mal', sagte Igor Strawinsky, 'dass es mir gelang, beim Erwachen eine im Traum deutlich gehörte musikalische Phrase ganz festzuhalten und aufzuschreiben, denn die musikalischen Träume verflüchtigen sich beim Erwachen.' Das Motiv der Zigeunerin wurde zum Tango in der *Geschichte vom Soldaten*. Laut Ankündigung sollte das Stück 'gelesen, gespielt und getanzt' werden. Die materiellen Schwierigkeiten der Zeit zwangen zur Sparsamkeit. Drei Tänzer-Schauspieler, ein Vorleser und sieben Musiker. Solche Voraussetzungen führten den Komponisten zur Schöpfung einer neuen musikalischen Sprache von absichtlicher Schlichtheit.

Vier Freunde trafen sich unter unserem Dach: Strawinsky, Ramuz, Ansermet und René Auberjonois; dieser entwarf Bühnenbilder und Kostüme. Am Familientisch war die väterliche Laune das treue Stimmungsbarometer dieser Zusammenkünfte, bei denen es oft hoch herging: schön, veränderlich, stürmisch . . . Aber Begeisterung herrschte bei der ganzen Vorbereitungsarbeit vor. Die Aufführung fand am 29. September 1918 in Lausanne statt. Sie verschaffte meinem Vater, wie er später selbst schrieb, die grösste Befriedigung, die er je bei der Aufführung eines seiner Bühnenwerke empfunden hatte.

Wie glücklich und stolz war ich vor meinen kleinen Schulkameraden, die aufgeputzt mit ihren Eltern in der Nachbarloge sassen. Und wie könnte ich hier, da es sich um Erinnerungen handelt, den unvergesslichen Vorleser Elie Gagnebin übergehen? Sein wahrhaft schauspielerisches Vorlesen begeisterte uns. Die treue Freundschaft, die ihn mit unserer ganzen Familie verband, begann mit der *Geschichte vom Soldaten*. Für die geplanten Tourneen war man an jenem Septemberende 1918 optimistisch eingestellt, und doch sollte diese Premiere während vieler Jahre die einzige Aufführung dieses Werkes bleiben! Die schreckliche Epidemie, die damals in ganz Europa unter dem Namen 'spanische Grippe' wütete, ergriff plötzlich Autoren, Schauspieler und Musiker . . . Alles musste sich ins Bett legen. Zuhause sehe ich meinen Vater tief unter seinen Decken vergraben, mit klappernden Zähnen, die Baskenmütze bis über die Augen gezogen, voller Ingrimm. Ich sehe meine Mutter im Schlafrock herumwanken, allen, gross und klein, Arzneien, Kräutertee, Sirup verabreichend . . . Die geplante Tournee fiel endgültig ins Wasser; das Werk aber sollte später anderswo und auf andere Weise seinen ruhmreichen Weg gehen.

Obwohl die *Geschichte vom Soldaten* unbestritten eines der Hauptwerke der Strawinskyschen Produktion ist, und Sergej Diagilev sicherlich einer der ersten Bewunderer meines Vaters war, grollte dieser Pionier, dieser Neuerer, dieser Mann mit der feinen Spürnase dem neuen Werk. Es stand nicht unter seiner Schutzherrschaft! Wollte das Lieblingsfohlen etwa aus seinem Stall ausbrechen?

Wir kommen nun zum letzten Jahr unseres Lebens in Morges. Der Krieg ist aus. Mein Vater reist immer häufiger nach Paris. In meiner Erinnerung bleibt diese Zeit von dem Hauptwerk beherrscht, an dem Strawinsky damals arbeitete: *Pulcinella*. Von einer seiner Reisen hatte er eine Sammlung unvollendeter Werke und ungedruckter Fragmente Pergolesis mitgebracht, ein Notenmaterial, das Diagilev aus verschiedenen Bibliotheken Europas zusammengelesen hatte, und das dem Komponisten die musikalische Basis für ein neues Ballet lieferte. Damals fiel im täglichen Leben der Familie Strawinsky immer häufiger der bereits berühmte Name Pablo Picasso. War dieser schon seit einigen Jahren ein Freund meines Vaters gewesen, so knüpften sich anlässlich des Ballets *Pulcinella*, für das er Bühnenbilder und Kostüme entwarf, zwischen dem Musiker und dem Maler engere Beziehungen. Wenn ein Trio wie das Diagilev-Strawinsky-Picassosche bei der Zusammenarbeit aufeinanderprallte, mussten unweigerlich Funken stieben, die einen ganzen Himmel in Flammen aufgehen lassen konnten. Aber das gegenseitige Vertrauen, das der Bewunderung dieser drei Grossen füreinander entsprang, überwand die Hindernisse und führte zu einem der grössten Erfolge des Russischen Ballets. Die Gestalt Picassos wurde uns damals vertraut; sie war zuhause durch eine Serie von Zeichnungen, von Gouaschen und Ölbildern verkörpert, die der Maler meinen Eltern geschenkt hatte. Dem berühmten Bleistiftporträt des Komponisten in Vorderansicht, mit der Widmung: 'für Strawinsky von seinem Freund Picasso', gab meine Mutter an unseren Wänden den Ehrenplatz.

So weit ich in meinen Kindheitserinnerungen zurückgehe, ich sehe mich nie anders als mit dem Wunsch, Maler zu werden, 'wenn ich gross bin'. Die Berührung mit dem Werk Picassos und bald mit seiner Person sollte für mich als wahres Reagens wirken. Bei meinen Eltern, die alle beide so empfänglich für die bildenden Künste waren, sowie bei ihren Malerfreunden stiess ich nur auf Ermunterung; meine Bahn war gezeichnet. Die meines Bruders sollte ihrerseits bald gezeichnet werden. Seit der frühesten Kindheit wollte Sulima Pianist werden, und mein Vater begrüsste diese unzweifelhafte Berufung. Sehr früh spielte der eigene Sohn Igor Strawinskys in der ganzen Welt unter anderem das Klavierrepertoire des Vaters. Aber greifen wir nicht vor . . . , es sei denn, um nebenbei zu bemerken, dass der Urenkel Feodor Ignatjevitsch Strawinskys, John, der Enkel Igors, der Sohn Sulimas, seinerseits eine wahre Schauspielerbegabung an den Tag legt . . .

Kehren wir nach Morges zurück, wir sind im Jahre 1920. Die internationalen Nachkriegsumstände eröffneten der glänzenden Laufbahn des noch jungen Künstlers, der mein Vater damals war, einen neuen Wirkungskreis. Er konnte sich nicht mehr mit unserer Wohnung in der entzückenden kleinen waadtländischen Stadt begnügen, wohin die Feindseligkeiten in der Welt unser Familienleben verbannt hatten. Nachdem sie eine Weile an Rom gedacht hatten, beschlossen meine Eltern, nach Paris zu übersiedeln. Zu den ohnehin schon zahlreichen Strawinskys kam nun die Familie meines Onkels Beljankin hinzu, der nach tausend Umwegen und Abenteuern Russland hatte verlassen und zu uns nach Morges hatte kommen können. Meine Mutter und meine Tante, die als Schwestern so sehr aneinander hingen, fanden endlich wieder zusammen, und wir Kinder hatten Vetter und Kusine wieder. So reiste mein Vater wieder einmal an der Spitze einer ganzen Sippe als wahrer Patriarch – den Bart jedoch trug mein Onkel! – mit seinen Leuten von Morges nach Paris, einer neuen Bestimmung entgegen . . .

Die Vorbereitungen zur Abreise waren, wie man sich wohl denken kann, keine Kleinigkeit. Mein Vater dachte an alles, machte sich überall zu schaffen; meine Mutter, unterstützt von Madubo, kümmerte sich ums Praktische; wir Kinder machten unsere Besuche, verabschiedeten uns von unseren Kameraden, von unseren Lehrern.

In der Wohnung des Maison Bornand ist ein einziges Drunter und Drüber. Koffer, Kisten, Stroh, Zugluft, Möbelträger und Weingläser. Statt auf Stühlen sitzt man auf Kisten und plaudert mit den Freunden, die nacheinander herbeieilen, um uns Lebewohl zu sagen. Ich höre: 'Also Ramuz, Sie kommen nicht mit?'. 'Aber Strawinsky, stellen Sie sich doch einmal vor! Paris, das ist furchtbar weit . . . , und ich bin kein Globe-Trotter wie Sie!'. Ein Ton, den Ramuz gern annahm . . .

Mit den Jahren wird es deutlich, dass man, wie ich es zu Beginn dieses Albums geschrieben habe, ohne allzu grosse Willkür das Leben meines Vaters in drei Abschnitte einteilen kann, deren erster ohne Zweifel an eben diesem Sommeranfang des Jahres 1920 zuende geht, da wir die Schweiz, Morges, verlassen.

Endlich ist der grosse Tag der Abreise da. Wir sind mehr als ein Dutzend, gross und klein, die sich in, ich weiss nicht wievielen, Coupés verteilen. Aufenthalt in Genf, wo man in einigen Stunden den Nachtzug nach Paris nehmen wird. Ansermets kommen, mit kleinen Geschenken beladen, zum Bahnhof. Und noch andere Freunde werden auf dem Bahnsteig mit dem Taschentuch winken. Bis zur Abreise isst man belegte Brote im Bahnhofsrestaurant. Den Kleinen gibt man Grenadine-Saft, aber mir schenkt mein Vater, der mich an jenem Tag wie einen Erwachsenen ansieht, mit Ernst mein erstes *richtiges Glas Bier* ein. Diese väterliche Geste sehe ich noch heute. Halten wir sie als eine der vielleicht letzten Erinnerungen an meine Kindheit fest. Ungweigerlich führt sie mich zur allerersten Erinnerung meiner allerfrühesten Kindheit zurück . . . Wieder einmal in den Annalen unserer Familie zählt man auf dem Bahnsteig wieder und wieder Pakete und Koffer, aber vor allem lässt man den einen nicht aus den Augen, den aus mehr als einem Grund gewichtigen, den allerkostbarsten, der die schon so zahlreichen Manuskripte Igor Strawinskys enthält.

Théodore Strawinsky

The birth of Igor Stravinsky.
On a calendar leaf of 5/18 June 1882 a note by his father:
'In the year 1882 on 5th June at noon our son Igor was born at Oranienbaum, rue de Suisse, villa Khoudvintzev. He was christened on 29th July of the same year.'
In the top right hand corner: Ghima, a nickname given to him by his parents when he was born and by which he was known to the rest of the family. Later on his wife Catherine never called him by any other name.

Naissance d'Igor Strawinsky.
Feuillet de calendrier annoté par son père à la date du 5/18 juin 1882.
'L'an 1882, le 5 juin à midi, naquit notre fils Igor à Oranienbaum, rue de Suisse, villa Khoudvintzev. Baptisé le 29 juillet de la même année.'
En haut à droite: Ghima, petit nom qui lui fut donné dès sa naissance par ses parents et qui lui resta parmi les siens. Plus tard, sa femme Catherine ne l'appellera jamais autrement.

Die Geburt Igor Strawinskys.
Auf dem Kalenderblatt vom 5/18. Juni 1882 eine Notiz seines Vaters:
'Im Jahre 1882, am 5. Juni zu Mittag wurde unser Sohn Igor in Oranienbaum, rue de Suisse, Villa Khoudvintzev, geboren. Er wurde am 29. Juli des selben Jahres getauft.'
Oben rechts: Ghima, ein Kosename, der ihm nach seiner Geburt von seinen Eltern gegeben wurde und ihm in seiner Familie dann blieb. Später nannte ihn auch seine Frau Katharina nie anders.

Fedor Ignatievich and Anna Kyrillovna,
the parents of Igor.
Odessa, 16th July 1874.

Feodor Ignatievitch et Anna Kyrillovna,
les parents d'Igor.
Odessa, 16 juillet 1874.

Feodor Ignatjewitsch und Anna
Kyrillowna, Igors Eltern.
Odessa, 16. Juli 1874.

Feodor Ignatievich Stravinsky in the part
of Makagonenko in Rimsky-Korsakov's
La Nuit de Mai

Feodor Ignatievitch Strawinsky dans le
rôle de Makagonenko dans *La Nuit de Mai*
de Rimsky-Korsakov.

Feodor Ignatjewitsch Strawinsky in der
Rolle des Makagonenko in Rimsky-
Korsakov's *La Nuit de Mai*

In his father's library.
Igor at his father's side; his mother; his
brothers Gouri and Roman.

Dans la bibliothèque paternelle.
Igor aux cotés de son père; sa mère;
ses frères Gouri et Roman.

In der väterlichen Bibliothek.
Igor neben seinem Vater; seine Mutter;
seine Brüder Guri und Roman.

Around the family table : Igor in the left
foreground.

Autour de la table familiale : Igor au
premier plan à gauche.

Um den Familientisch : Igor links im
Vordergrund.

Igor in his student's uniform: law . . .   Igor en uniforme d'étudiant: le droit . . .   Igor in seiner Studentenuniform: Jura . . .

... and music   ... et la musique   ... und Musik

Drawing by Igor 1901.   Dessin d'Igor 1901.   Zeichnung Igors 1901.

The young student sometimes draws   Parfois le jeune étudiant dessine   Der junge Student zeichnet manchmal

Roman, Igor's eldest brother poses.
Catherine Nossenko (on the right) and
their cousin Olga paint. 1902.

Roman, frère aîné d'Igor pose.
Catherine Nossenko (à droite) et leur
cousine Olga peignent. 1902.

Roman, Igors ältester Bruder sitzt Modell.
Katharina Nossenko (rechts) und ihre
Kusine Olga malen. 1902.

Igor at the piano. Behind him his brother
Youri and their first cousin Catherine
Nossenko.

Igor au piano. Derrierè lui son frère Youri
et leur cousine germaine Catherine
Nossenko.

Igor am Klavier. Hinter ihm sein Bruder
Juri und ihre Kusine Katharina Nossenko.

Catherine and Ludmila Nossenko on the right. Their cousins Olga and Vera Nossenko on the left. Paris 1903.

Catherine et Ludmila Nossenko à droite. Leurs cousines Olga et Véra Nossenko à gauche. Paris 1903.

Katharina und Ludmilla Nossenko rechts. Ihre Kusinen Olga und Vera Nossenko links. Paris 1903.

Ludmila marries a naval officer.

Ludmila Nossenko épousera un officier de marine.

Ludmilla heiratet einen Marineoffizier

The two sisters Catherine and Ludmila.   Les deux soeurs Catherine et Ludmila.   Die beiden Schwestern Katharina und
Ludmilla.

Igor and his brother Gouri.   Igor et son frère Gouri.   Igor und sein Bruder Guri.

The engagement.
Note in Igor's handwriting:
'Photographed at Omelno a few hours
before we became engaged. 14th August
1905.
Signed Catherine & Igor.

Les fiançailles.
Annotation de la main d'Igor:
'Photographiés à Omelno, quelques heures
avant que nous devenions fiancés.
14 aôut 1905.'
Signé Catherine & Igor.

Die Verlobung.
Handschriftlicher Vermerk Igors:
'Diese Photographie wurde in Omelno
einige Stunden vor unserer Verlobung
gemacht. 14. August 1905.
Unterschrift Katharina & Igor.

The young married couple.
St Petersburg 1906.

Les jeunes mariés.
St Petersbourg 1906.

Das junge Paar.
St Petersburg 1906.

Igor and Catherine with Ludmila and
Gouri at Oustiloug.

Igor et Catherine avec Ludmila et Gouri à
Oustiloug.

Igor und Katharina mit Ludmilla und
in Ustilug.

Family group at St Petersburg.　　　En famille à St Petersbourg.　　　Familienphoto in St Petersburg.

Igor and Catherine after the birth of their first child Theodore.

Igor et Catherine après la naissance de leur premier né Théodore.

Igor und Katharina nach der Geburt ihres ersten Kindes, Theodor.

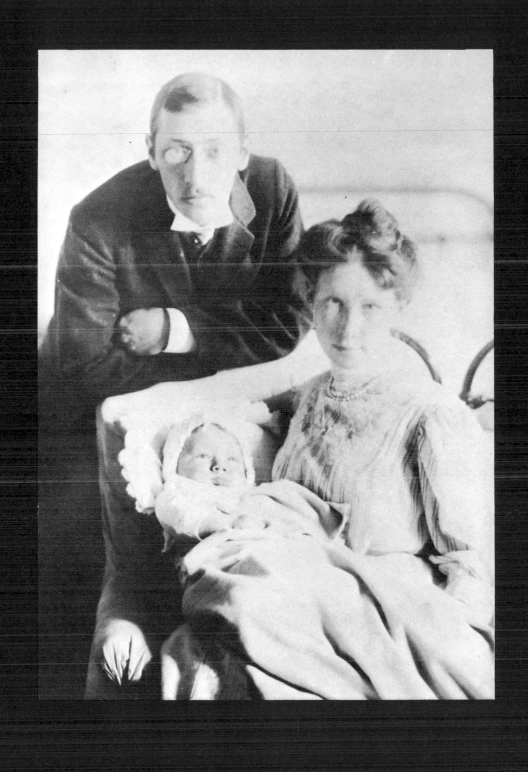

Igor and Catherine with their son
Theodore. 1907.

Igor et Catherine avec leur fils Théodore.
1907.

Igor und Katharina mi
Theodor. 1907.

The rural summer residence of the young couple at Oustiloug.

La demeure rurale et estivale du jeune couple à Oustiloug.

Der ländliche Sommersitz des jungen Paares in Ustilug.

On the porch at Oustiloug:
Igor takes down the song of a blind moujik.
On the right: his mother with her
grandson Theodore on the lap.

Sur le perron d'Oustiloug:
Igor note le chant d'un moujik aveugle.
A droite: sa mère, tenant sur ses genoux
son petit-fils Théodore.

Beim Aufgang in Ustilug:
Igor schreibt den Gesang eines blinden
Mujik nieder. Rechts davon: seine Mutter
mit ihrem Enkel Theodor auf den Knien.

Catherine and her eldest child.   Catherine avec son aîné.   Katharina und ihr Ältester.

After the triumph of the *Firebird*.
La Baule. 1910.
From left to right: two nannies,
Catherine, Igor and his mother.
In the foreground: Mika (Ludmila)
and Theodore.

Après le triomphe de *l'Oiseau de Feu*.
La Baule. 1910.
De gauche à droite: deux nianias,
Catherine, Igor et sa mère.
Au premier plan: Mika (Ludmila)
et Théodore

Nach dem Triumph des *Feuervogel*.
La Baule. 1910.
Von links nach rechts: zwei Njanjas
Katharina, Igor und seine Mutter.
Im Vordergrund: Mika (Ludmilla) und
Theodor.

Igor and Catherine, La Baule.   Igor et Catherine, La Baule.   Igor und Katharina, La Baule.

Igor to his mother. 1911:
'from Beaulieu where your son is working

Igor à sa mère. 1911:
'de Beaulieu où ton fils travaille à

Igor an seine Mutter. 1911:
'von Beaulieu, wo Dein Sohn an

Igor and Catherine with their cousin Vera
Nossenko at Omelno (Russia). 1911.

Igor et Catherine avec leur cousine Véra
Nossenko à Omelno (Russie). 1911.

Igor und Katharina mit ihrer Kusine Vera
Nossenko in Omelno (Russland). 1911.

Oustiloug. 1912.
In those years the Japanese engravings
are taking the place of honour on the
young composer's walls.

Oustiloug. 1912. En ces années-là les
estampes japonaises ont, sur les murs du
jeune compositeur, la place d'honneur.

Ustilug. 1912.
In jenen Jahren sind es die japanischen
Holzschnitte, die den Ehrenplatz auf den
Wänden des jungen Komponisten

Clarens, Pension 'les Tilleuls'. 1912.
At this beautiful Swiss 18th Century table
Igor Stravinsky is working on the *Rite of
Spring*.

Clarens, Pension 'les Tilleuls'. 1912.
Sur cette belle table suisse XVIIIe
Igor Strawinsky travaille au *Sacre*.

Clarens, Pension 'les Tilleuls'. 1912.
An diesem schönen Schweizer Tisch aus
dem 18. Jahrhundert arbeitet Igor
Strawinsky an seinem *Frühlingsopfer*.

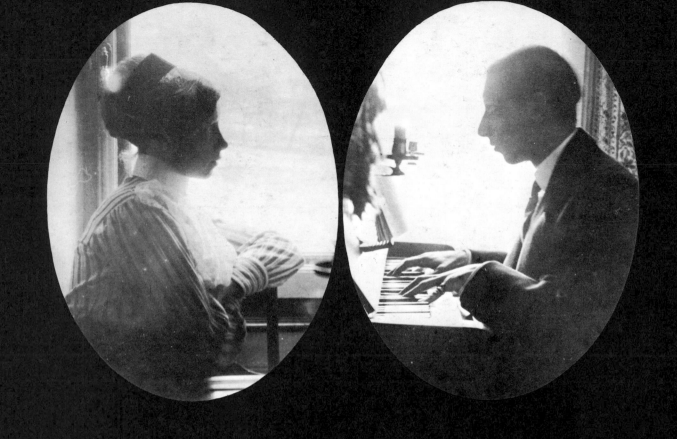

Catherine and Igor, Clarens. 1912.   Catherine et Igor, Clarens. 1912.   Katharina und Igor, Clarens. 1912.

Catherine and her daughter Ludmila on the shores of Lake Geneva.

Catherine avec sa fille Ludmila sur les rives du Léman.

Katharina und ihre Tochter Ludmilla an den Ufern des Genfer Sees.

Igor smoked a pipe on rare occasions.   Igor ne fumera que rarement la pipe.   Igor rauchte nur selten eine Pfeife.

Clarens. 1913.
Catherine, Igor and their three children
with Baba Sonia, Catherine's nanny.

Clarens. 1913.
Catherine, Igor et leur trois enfants avec
Baba Sonia, la niania de Catherine.

Clarens. 1913.
Katharina, Igor und ihre drei Kinder mit
Baba Sonia, Katharinas Njanja.

Oustiloug, 1913
The three Stravinsky children with their
cousin Ira Belyankin on the left and her
brother Gania on the right.

Oustiloug, 1913
Les trois enfants Strawinsky avec leur
cousine Ira Beliankine à gauche et son
frère Gania à droite.

Ustilug, 1913
Die drei Strawinsky-Kinder mit ihrer
Kusine Ira Beljankin links und deren
Bruder Ganja rechts.

The family at Oustiloug:
Catherine with her son Theodore, Anna
Stravinsky and, to her left, her son Gouri
and Bertha Essert, the faithful nanny of
Igor and his brothers.

En famille à Oustiloug:
Catherine avec son fils Théodore, Anna
Strawinsky avec, à ses cotés, son fils Gouri,
Bertha Essert la fidele niania d'Igor et de
ses frères.

Die Familie in Ustilug:
Katharina mit ihrem Sohn Theodor, Anna
Strawinsky, und ihr zur Seite ihr Sohn Guri
sowie Bertha Essert, die getreue Njanja
von Igor und seinen Brüdern.

In 1913 Igor already has three children.   En 1913 Igor a déjà trois enfants.   1913 hat Igor bereits drei Kinder.

Igor and his two eldest children at Oustiloug.

Igor avec ses deux ainés à Oustiloug.

Igor mit seinen beiden ältesten Kindern in Ustilug.

Catherine with her two eldest children in Oustiloug.

Catherine avec ses deux ainés à Oustiloug.

Katharina mit ihren beiden ältesten Kindern in Ustilug.

The mother of Igor, Anna Kyrillovna, with her three grand-children in a corner of the garden at Oustiloug. 1913.

La mère d'Igor, Anna Kyrillovna avec ses trois petits-enfants dans un coin du jardin d'Oustiloug. 1913.

Igors Mutter, Anna Kyrillowna, mit ihren drei Enkeln in einer Ecke des Gartens in Ustilug. 1913.

Also at Oustiloug : Igor's study.
From left to right : His mother, Bertha, his
wife and his sister-in-law. On the wall at
the right his father's portrait and over the
bookcase Pushkin's.

Toujours à Oustiloug : le cabinet de
travail d'Igor.
De gauche à droite : Sa mère, Bertha, sa
femme et sa belle-soeur. Au mur à droite
le portrait de son père. Au-dessus de la
bibliothèque celui de Pouchkine.

Noch immer in Ustilug : Igors
Arbeitszimmer.
Von links nach rechts : Seine Mutter,
Bertha, seine Frau und seine Schwägerin.
Rechts an der Wand ein Bild seines
Vaters. Über dem Bücherschrank eines
von Puschkin.

1913. Clarens, Hotel du Châtelard.
On Igor's left, his wife. Standing: their
niece Ira, their daughter Ludmila next to
their cousin Vera Nossenko. On the right:
their sister-in-law and sister Ludmila
Belyankin.

1913. Clarens, Hôtel du Châtelard.
A la gauche d'Igor, sa femme. Debout:
leur nièce Ira, leur fille Ludmila auprès de
Vera Nossenko leur cousine. A droite: leur
belle-soeur et soeur Ludmila Beliankine.

1913. Clarens, Hotel du Châtelard.
Links von Igor, seine Frau. Stehend: ihre
Nichte Ira, ihre Tochter Ludmilla neben
ihrer Kusine Vera Nossenko. Rechts: ihre
Schwägerin und Schwester Ludmilla
Beljankin.

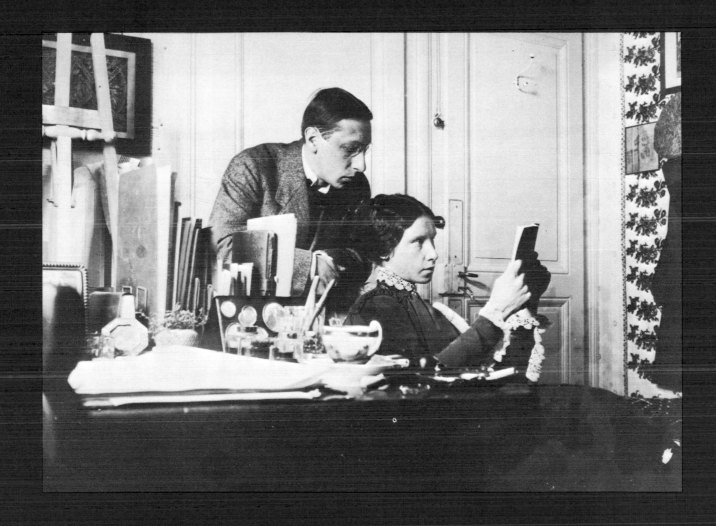

Also at the 'Châtelard'.
The Study.

Toujours au 'Châtelard'.
Le cabinet de travail.

Wiederum im 'Châtelard'.
Das Arbeitszimmer.

Igor at Clarens. 1914.   Igor à Clarens. 1914.   Igor in Clarens. 1914.

Catherine with her last-born child Milena –
with note by Igor.

Catherine avec sa dernière-née Milène –
Annotation d'Igor.

Katharina mit ihrer Letztgeborenen,
Milena – mit Vermerk Igors.

Igor, the attentive father . . . Salvan.   Igor, père attentif . . . Salvan.   Igor, der aufmerksame Vater . . . Salvan.

General mobilisation of the Swiss army.
Note from Igor: 'Drawing by Theo
Stravinsky, August 1914. Salvan.'

Mobilisation générale de l'armée suisse.
Annotation d'Igor: 'Dessiné par Théo
Strawinsky, août 1914. Salvan.'

Generalmobilisierung der Schweizer
Armee. Vermerk Igors: 'Gezeichnet von
Theo Strawinsky, August 1914. Salvan.'

Clarens, 'la Pervenche'.
Milena on her father's knees at the time
when Igor Stravinsky started work on
Les Noces. 1915.

Clarens, 'la Pervenche'.
Milène sur les genoux de son père à l'epoque
où Igor Strawinsky ébauche *les Noces*.
1915.

Clarens, 'la Pervenche'.
Milena auf den Knien des Vaters, zur
Zeit, als Igor Strawinsky mit *Der Hochzeit*
begann. 1915.

Soulima with his mother at 'la Pervenche'.   Soulima auprès de sa mère à' la Pervenche'.   Soulima mit seiner Mutter in 'la Pervenche'.

Bertha was our nanny just as she was our
father's.

Bertha fut notre niania, comme elle avait
été celle de notre père.

Bertha war unsere Njanja, wie sie auch
schon die unseres Veters gewesen war.

In the garden Igor's breakfast.   Au jardin le petit déjeuner d'Igor.   Im Garten Igors Frühstück.

Igor and his four children.   Igor et ses quatre enfants.   Igor und seine vier Kinder.

The Krioukov Canal at St. Petersburg, later called Leningrad. On the second floor, above the entrance, are the windows of the apartment which was occupied for more than eighty years by the Stravinsky family . . .

Canal Krioukov à St. Petersbourg qui deviendra Leningrad. Au 2e étage au-dessus du porche, les fenêtres de l'appartement qui fut habité plus de quatre-vingt ans par des générations de Strawinsky . . .

Der Krioukov Kanal in St. Petersburg, dem späteren Leningrad. Im zweiten Stock, über dem Eingang, kann man die Fenster der Wohnung sehen, die während mehr als 80 Jahren von Stravinskys bewohnt wurde . . .

... the intrepid Gouri lived there with his mother until 1915 when he left for the Balkan Front.

... l'intrépide Gouri qui y vivait avec sa mère s'engage, en 1915, sur le front des Balkans.

... der unerschrockene Guri wohnte dort mit seiner Mutter, bis er sich 1915 an die Balkanfront meldete.

Morges, 1915.

Soulima already playing the piano.

Morges, 1915.

Soulima déjà au piano.

Morges, 1915.

Soulima spielt schon Klavier.

A summer's day.　　　　　　　Journée d'été.　　　　　　　Ein Sommertag.

In front of the 'Villa Rogivue', Morges.
1916.

Devant la 'Villa Rogivue', Morges. 1916.

Vor der 'Villa Rogivue', Morges. 1916.

At the same period :
Igor and his four children.

A la même époque :
Igor avec ses quatre enfants.

Zur selben Zeit :
Igor und seine vier Kinder.

Igor and his son Soulima in the park at
Morges . . .

Igor avec son fils Soulima dans le parc de
Morges . . .

Igor und sein Sohn Sulima im Park von
Morges . . .

. . . and in front of the little harbour. . . . et devant le petit port. . . . und vor dem kleinen Hafen.

Mina Switalski, our dear 'Madubo', becomes our nanny and a member of our family. 1917.

Mina Switalski, notre cherè 'Madubo', entre dans la famille et devient notre niania. 1917.

Mina Switalski, unsere liebe 'Madubo' wird unsere Njanja und ein Teil unserer Familie. 1917.

Les Diablerets, summer 1917.   Les Diablerets, été 1917.   Les Diablerets, Sommer 1917.

Les Diablerets. Igor working on the
joiner's bench. Next to him, as always, the
same photographs : his wife, his parents,
his teacher, his children. On the wall the
Picasso sketches for the Russian Ballet.

Les Diablerets. Igor travaille sur l'établi
du menuisier. Auprès de lui toujours les
mêmes photographies : sa femme, ses
parents, son maître, ses enfants. Au mur
des maquettes de Picasso pour les Ballets
Russes.

Les Diablerets. Igor arbeitet auf der
Hobelbank. Um ihn sind wie immer die
selben Photographien : seine Frau, seine
Eltern, sein Lehrer, seine Kinder. An
der Wand sind die Picasso Entwürfe für
das Russische Ballett.

Catherine sitting in the doorway of the workshop.

Catherine assise à la porte de l'atelier.

Katharina sitzt im Eingang zur Werkstatt.

In a boat on Lake Geneva. 1919.
Catherine and her two daughters.

En barque sur le lac Léman. 1919.
Catherine et ses deux filles.

Im Boot auf dem Genfer See. 1919.
Katharina und ihre beiden Töchter.

Igor and his brother-in-law Gregory
Belyankin.

Igor et son beau-frère Grégoire
Beliankine.

Igor und sein Schwager Gregor
Beljankin.

The Stravinskys are leaving Switzerland. This photograph was in Father's passport. 1920.

Les Strawinsky vont quitter la Suisse. Cette photographie sur le passeport paternel. 1920.

Die Strawinskys verlassen die Schweiz. Diese Photographie befand sich im väterlichen Reisepass. 1920.

'Maison Bornand', where the *Soldier's Tale* and *Pulcinella* were composed, was the Stravinsky home between 1917 and 1920. Before leaving Morges Igor takes a last photograph with Catherine at the window.

La 'maison Bornand', où furent composés *l'Histoire du Soldat* et *Pulcinella* abrita les Strawinsky de 1917 à 1920. Avant de quitter Morges Igor prend une dernière photographie avec Catherine à la fenêtre.

Zwischen 1917 und 1920 wohnten die Strawinskys im 'Haus Bornand', wo die *Geschichte vom Soldaten* und *Pulcinella* komponiert wurden. Vor der Abreise von Morges macht Igor noch ein letztes Photo mit Katharina am Fenster.

Igor and Theodore Stravinsky.   Igor et Théodore Strawinsky.   Igor und Theodor Strawinsky.

Pour mon fils
— Theodore
et pour jouer sur sa
transposée en MI
une petite mélodie

Son père
IStr

Le 24 Mars 1912

Epilogue

In June 1970, Igor Stravinsky was brought by his wife Vera and
Robert Craft, a musician who was living with them, from New York
to Evian, on the French side of the Lake of Geneva. They stayed there
until September. Since we lived in Geneva, we were able to see my
father every day for more than two months, and my wife took a
number of touching photographs of the invalid we cherished. Five of
them will act as epilogue to our album.
The first shows the hotel-window through which Igor Stravinsky
can be seen sitting motionless in his armchair. And by a deeply
moving chance, we can see superimposed on the last picture of him
by the reflexion on the window-pane, the Swiss side of the lake
where he lived in his young days – Clarens, Lausanne, Morges . . .
But what can memories weigh in the face of Eternity? The second: a
conversation that was to be perhaps the last we had together . . .
Then his wonderful hands. Finally, as an end-piece, a poignant
moment of recollection.

Epilogue

En juin 1970 Igor Strawinsky fut amené par sa femme Vera et par
Robert Craft, musicien qui vivait avec eux, de New York à Evian,
sur le versant français du lac Léman. Ils y restèrent jusqu'à
septembre. Ma femme et moi habitant Genève, eûmes ainsi durant
plus de deux mois la possibilité de voir mon père quotidiennement.
Mon épouse prit du cher grand malade toute une série
d'émouvantes photographies. En voici cinq qui serviront
d'épilogue à notre album.
La première : cette fenêtre d'hôtel, derrière laquelle on distingue
Igor Strawinsky, immobile dans son fauteuil. Fenêtre dont la vitre
nous renvoie, par-dessus sa dernière image – bouleversante
rencontre – le reflet des rives qu'il habita dans sa jeunesse : la côte
suisse. Clarens, Lausanne, Morges . . . Mais de quel poids les
souvenirs peuvent-ils être face à l'Eternité?
La seconde : un échange de paroles qui sera peut-être entre nous le
dernier . . . Ensuite ses admirables mains. Enfin, pour clore ces pages,
un regard intérieur poignant.

Epilog

Im Juni 1970 wurde Igor Strawinsky von seiner Frau Vera und
Robert Craft, einem Musiker der bei ihnen lebte, von New York nach
Evian gebracht, auf der französischen Seite des Genfersees. Dort
blieben sie bis September. Da wir in Genf wohnten, konnten wir so
meinen Vater während mehr als zwei Monaten täglich sehen, und
meine Frau machte von dem teuren, grossen Kranken eine ganze
Reihe ergreifender Photographien. Fünf dieser Aufnahmen bilden
den Epilog unseres Albums.
Die erste : jenes Hotelfenster, hinter dem man Igor Strawinsky
unbeweglich in seinem Sessel sehen kann. Ein Fenster, in dessen
Scheibe sich über seinem letzten Bild – ergreifende Begegnung – die
Ufer widerspiegeln, die er in seiner Jugend bewohnte : die
Schweizer Seeseite. Clarens, Lausanne, Morges . . . Doch was weigen
Erinnerungen im Vergleich zur Ewigkeit? Die zweite : ein
Gespräch, das vielleicht unser letztes sein sollte . . . Dann seine
wunderbaren Hände. Zuletzt, als Abschluss dieser Seiten, ein
schmerzlicher, verinnerlichter Blick.

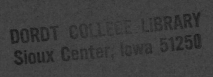